DEVELOPING NEIGHBOURHOOD SUPPORT AND CHILD PROTECTION STRATEGIES

For mothers in the Henley Ward
- and parents everywhere - who struggle against the odds to give
their children a good start in life

Developing Neighbourhood Support and Child Protection Strategies

The Henley Safe Children Project

NORMA BALDWIN
LYN CARRUTHERS

With good wishes —

Norma

Ashgate

Aldershot • Brookfield USA • Singapore • Sydney

Published by
Ashgate Publishing Ltd
Gower House
Croft Road
Aldershot
Hants GU11 3HR
England

Ashgate Publishing Company
Old Post Road
Brookfield
Vermont 05036
USA

British Library Cataloguing in Publication Data
Baldwin, Norma, 1939 -
    Developing neighbourhood support and child protection
    strategies: the henley safe children project
    1. Children - Services for - England - Henley
    I. Title II. Carruthers, Lyn
    362.7'1'0942498

Library of Congress Catalog Card Number: 98-72850

ISBN 1 84014 312 6

Printed and bound by Athenaeum Press, Ltd.,
Gateshead, Tyne & Wear.

Contents

Tables

Figures

Acknowledgments

We should like to thank the following individuals and agencies for resources, ideas and materials which were helpful in developing the work of the Henley Safe Children Project, the New Links Project and in writing the book.

Parents and workers in the Wood End and Bell Green areas of the Henley Ward. For planning, writing and effective delivery in the dissemination of parents' views — Elaine O'Brien, Nicki Moore, Sam O'Connor, Mandy Watson.

Home Office Safer Cities Project — in particular Margaret Geary. The NSPCC. Sue Fallon, formerly of the NSPCC.

Coventry City Council and Social Services Department. Allen Torrance and members of the Policy, Research and Planning Sections of Coventry Social Services Department. Workers from the northeast team of the Community Education section for support, access and co-work. Carol Hayden and Sarah Holmes of the Wood End Area Management Team.

Freddie Lewis, Locality Manager, Health Authority. Nick Spencer, University of Warwick.

For census information and statistics — the Economic Development Department, Coventry City Council. For help with mapping — Kris and Paul Benington. For presentation of maps and figures — Gina Finlayson, Town & Regional Planning, University of Dundee.

For endless patience with word processing of drafts, reports and the book — Shelley Arthers of the NSPCC, Rhona Goodall and Judy Ahola, University of Dundee.

Responsibility for the material in the final form, for interpretation and opinion, remains with the authors.

Introduction

A theme of this book is that commitment to promote the wellbeing of children demands a detailed analysis of the range of factors which affect their life chances, at societal, neighbourhood, organisational and interpersonal levels. It demands a style of working which acknowledges this complexity and searches for solutions which reflect it in their objectives, principles and process. Such an approach is longterm, painstaking. It depends on agreed interagency strategies which involve local people in planning, implementation and evaluation.

At the end of the 1980s and beginning of the 1990s, following numerous inquiries into child deaths and serious incidents of child abuse, resources for child care were increasingly directed towards investigations of child abuse. Individual crisis work came to dominate child care services.

This book documents attempts in one area of Coventry to resist pressure to subsume all work with children and families under narrowly conceptualised child protection work. It is concerned with *what* is needed to support families; *why* it is needed; *how* it can best be provided.

The Henley Safe Children Project was set up in response to concerns by social workers, health care professionals, educationalists and social work educators and researchers, that individualised crisis work and child protection investigations were increasingly taking attention and resources away from neighbourhood family support and preventive work. The strong demonstrated links between disadvantage and many aspects of harm to children — including abuse, neglect, poor school achievements and crime — provided its rationale. The project was based on a commitment to work in partnership with parents, recognising them as experts on their own situations, to explore their views about keeping their children safe and to encourage agencies and individual professionals to give greater priority to family support and preventive work.

Since the Henley Project was set up, there has been a welcome change of emphasis in work with children and families, towards a much closer attention to ways in which families can be supported and harm prevented.

There have been changes in social policy, nationally and locally. A greater willingness to acknowledge the connections between individual needs and experience and wider economic and social factors is now apparent. European emphases on preventing social exclusion support this changing climate.

We hope that our account of experience in trying to work in this way — however modest in its scope and achievements — will be of benefit to policy makers, managers and social workers as they continue their efforts to develop children's services plans which will promote wellbeing for all children, refocusing services for the millenium.

A lot of the material in the book comes directly from parents struggling in difficult circumstances to bring up their children in health and safety. Their energy, successes, commitment and wisdom, as well as their failures, can teach us all a great deal

> We have the same fears as professionals for our children — we also have the same expectations for them as everyone else does. We have found that people do care about children but we need support to carry on caring. We want to help professionals to help us.

> We all have a responsibility to make children safe.

From Henley Safe Children Project Summary Report 1993 Keeping children safe: a responsibility for us all.

> Since we began talking to policy makers, attitudes about parents living on this estate have changed. Two years ago we were told that it would be impossible to have a safe play area built on the estate. Now the local authority have identified £200,000 to build one in consultation with local parents and children. The local authority have also shown a commitment to providing child care, and to ensure that meetings on service provision are scheduled at times that parents can attend. The NSPCC has responded positively to our views by providing our area with a coordinator and administration time for the New Links Project which is building on the work of the Henley Safe Children Project ... providing support to local parents, particularly those more likely to be isolated, through a network of trained 'parent volunteers'.

Elaine O'Brien, Nicki Moore, Sam O'Connor, Mandy Watson —Henley Safe Children Project: Letter to NSPCC.

Chapter one sets out the context of child protection and family support. It emphasises the known links between disadvantage, high child protection referrals and a range of harm to children. It describes some preventive schemes which have attempted to take account of these links.

Chapter two sets out the background to the Henley Safe Children Project and some of the characteristics of the area. It describes how information was gathered and used in the project.

Chapter three gives a detailed account of parents views and experience of trying to bring up children in a severely disadvantaged neighbourhood.

Chapter four gives the views of workers in the area about the needs of children and families.

Chapter five discusses the principles of partnership and community development on which the project was based. It considers how important the attention given to the *process* of the work was for the project and its outcomes.

Chapter six describes local activities initiated or supported by the development worker and parents from the Henley Safe Children Project and other local work in which they were involved. It draws out the implications of the project's findings and experience. It stresses the need for further development of planned interagency strategies of:

- neighbourhood and family support
- action with young people for a safer environment
- principles of partnership with communities
- positive action to build on the strengths of families and communities, drawing on their own resources and expertise.

1 The context of childcare and protection

This chapter considers the wider context within which the Henley Project was planned and developed. It discusses known links between high child protection referrals, other evidence of harm to children and aspects of disadvantage. Policy and legislation which fosters an active approach to preventive work, family support and promoting wellbeing is referred to. Some approaches which have had success in preventing harm and the principles on which they have been based are discussed. The value of community wide, interdisciplinary strategies is emphasised.

Links between disadvantage and harm to children

The social and economic circumstances of substantial minorities of families are associated with difficulties in bringing up children in health and safety. Childcare problems including high child protection referrals, are common in areas where there are high crime rates, poor school attendance, under achievement, drug use, teenage pregnancies. (Wilson and Herbert 1978; Brown and Madge 1982; Wedge and Essen 1982; Brown 1982; Becker and MacPherson 1988; Chamberlin 1988; Bebbington and Miles 1991; Blackburn 1991; Baldwin and Spencer 1993; Sedlak 1993; Spencer 1996; Reading 1997; Parton 1997). All these problems are associated with major social and economic disadvantages. Family breakdown and stress are closely linked to multiple deprivations in income, employment, housing, education and health (Court report 1976; NCB 1987 and 1992; Chamberlin 1988; Schorr 1988; DoH 1992; Graham 1993). Loneliness, stress, social isolation and vulnerability to mental health problems are particularly common for women with young children (Blackburn 1991) and are also associated with disadvantage.

Infant mortality in the United Kingdom is higher than in most other European countries and inequalities in children's health are substantial (NCH 1992; Spencer 1996; Reading 1997). High rates of low birth weight, infant mortality and poor health outcomes within countries are concentrated in the groups and regions with lowest incomes.

Children between 1 and 15 years in England and Wales are twice as likely to die in social classes IV and V as in I and II (Blackburn 1991). In England and Wales:

> Out of every 1000 babies born into social class V, 9.9 were stillborn or died in the first week of life, compared with 6.7 out of every 1000 babies born in social class I. Out of every 1000 babies born in social class V, 8.3 died in

their first year of life, compared with 4.6 out of every 1000 babies born in social class I. (NCH 1997 p.77).

Not all parents are assigned a social class in official figures, for example, single mothers who have never had a job. Reading draws attention to the implications of this for the real social differences:

> In 1993 infant mortality in the most affluent class (married, social class I) was 4.3/1000, whereas in the poorest class (unmarried, social class 'other') it was 18.3/1000 (Reading 1997 p.463)

Inequalities in child health are greater in countries with wide differences in income — such as the USA — than in countries where there are narrower differences in income between social classes — such as Sweden, the Netherlands and Denmark (Reading 1997, p. 464)

There are also striking differences across Europe in the availability of publicly funded childcare services, which might be seen as providing a measure of support for families and children, and which are associated with educational and other advantages in later life (New and David 1985). Between 35 and 40% of children aged 3-5 years have access to publicly funded childcare services in the UK, compared with 85% in Denmark and more than 95% in France and Belgium (NCH 1992).

There is a close correspondence between disadvantage and many aspects of harm to children (Schorr 1988; Utting 1993 and 1995; Baldwin and Spencer 1993; Roberts et al. 1995; Tennant 1995). Following major studies into possible 'cycles of deprivation' Brown and Madge (1982), concluded that the evidence showed that various aspects of harm and social and educational disadvantage were closely connected with the limitations imposed by adverse economic circumstances. The effects of adverse economic circumstances may persist over generations (Brown and Madge 1982; Brown 1983).

In their study of the circumstances of children who come into public care, Bebbington and Miles (1989) showed huge discrepancies between the likelihood of children in advantaged circumstances and those in disadvantaged circumstances coming into care.

Table 1   Likelihood of children in different circumstances coming into the care of the local authority

Child 'A' (aged 5-9)	Child 'B' (aged 5-9)
No supplementary benefit	Household head receives SB
Two parent family	Single adult household
Three or fewer children	Four or more children
White	Mixed ethnic origin
Owner occupied home	Private rented home
More rooms than people	One or more persons per room
<u>Odds are 1 in 7,000</u>	<u>Odds are 1 in 10</u>

(Bebbington and Miles 1989)

They also showed that living in areas with high rates of poverty had an independent influence, over and above that related to individual circumstances.

In Strathclyde 78% of children who came into care between 1985 — 92 were from families on benefits (Tennant 1995).

The fact that children of mixed racial heritage are exceptionally likely to come into care may reflect inordinate stresses within family groups where the racism, prejudice and inequality common within society enter into every aspect of life. It may also be connected with discriminatory processes and attitudes of agencies and professionals with responsibility for assessing the needs of children. More research is needed in this area. Meanwhile, it would appear that particular attention is needed to provide support for such families, in ways which will avoid stigma.

Black families are particularly likely to suffer material disadvantages and social injustice and to have to cope with added stresses because of individualised prejudice, harassment and abuse (Devore and Sclesinger 1987; Blackburn 1991; Cook and Watt 1992).

The Booths' study (1994) showed that mothers and fathers with learning disabilities are particularly vulnerable to intervention in their lives and the removal of their children from home. They too are likely to be materially disadvantaged.

NSPCC figures for the circumstances of children on child protection registers show very strong correlations between economic disadvantage and registration for child abuse and neglect. The forms used for registering children asked for approximate weekly income of families, but this was recorded for less than a quarter of those registered, so was not analysed. However, *over half of all the registered children's families were recorded as in receipt of supplementary benefit. Over three quarters of the cases registered for neglect and failure to thrive were in receipt of benefit.* (NSPCC 1987). In 1990, only 13% of mothers of children registered were in paid employment. Where there was a father in the family, 40% were unemployed (NSPCC 1990).

The percentage of parents whose employment status put them into the higher social class categories used by the Registrar General was so low that figures were combined in the NSPCC analysis. Social classes I and II were combined with the non manual occupations of class III. Only 4% of mothers of children registered were in this combined group, and only 5% of fathers. 1% of mothers and 11% of fathers were in occupations classified as Social Class 3 — manual. Compared with the population generally, semiskilled and unskilled occupations were heavily over represented. Debts were recorded for 25% of families on the registers. Of those registered for failure to thrive and neglect, 45% were recorded as having debts. (NSPCC 1987 and 1990) Some of the poorest families (Reading 1997) do not appear in a category at all — as mentioned under aspects of health and mortality earlier.

In a comprehensive study of the circumstances of children on Child Abuse Registers in America (Sedlak 1991 and 1993), low income was a powerful variable associated with abuse of all kinds. High income was a protective factor (Pelton 1994).

Interpretation of the data is complicated by the methods of collection, differing definitions of what constitutes abuse and neglect and the policing and social control role of professional childcare agencies. Nevertheless, the association between disadvantage and harm to children is so strong as to suggest that attention to economic factors is crucial in planning child protection strategies (Baldwin and Spencer 1993; Melton and Barry 1994; Parton 1997). When the individual harm suffered by children who are placed on child protection registers is looked at in parallel with other aspects of harm — ill health, poor school attainment, crime, drug abuse — associated with the disadvantaged neighbourhoods in which most of them live, the multiple chances of harm for some children become strikingly clear. In our view, these figures support the claim that adverse economic circumstances and the problems of living with inadequate resources severely limit the capacity of families to provide a nurturing and protective environment for their children. They raise questions about whether children in such families and neighbourhoods should be considered as 'in need' or 'at risk of significant harm' under the Children Act 1989, and Children Scotland Act 1995 (Baldwin and Spencer 1993; Melton and Barry 1994; Tuck 1995 and forthcoming; Sinclair et al. 1997).

In drawing attention to some of the statistics showing links between harm to children and aspects of disadvantage, we want to take care not to stereotype and further stigmatise disadvantaged groups. Whilst asking questions about the resources needed for families to provide a healthy environment, we want to pay attention to the strengths, skills and commitment of families and be aware of differences in family values, patterns of child rearing and cultural and religious priorities. Our approach to families as experts on their own situations is based on respect for difference and a view that families want the best for their children (Wilson and Herbert 1978; Mayall 1986; Blackburn 1991), without denying that serious harm can and does take place within families. The principles of the United Nations Convention and the Children Acts allow attention to be paid to the interconnected needs of children and families, without deviating from a commitment to the child's welfare as paramount and without allowing a 'rule of optimism' (Dingwall et al. 1988) to obscure potentially conflicting interests. The Henley Project was concerned to bring together the views of parents living in an area of disadvantage, about what would be helpful in protecting children, with knowledge gained from other projects which had been successful in preventing harm, to move toward positive strategies for services to children and families in the neighbourhood. We started from an ecological approach, seeing the child and family within wider social and economic contexts (Garbarino and Sherman 1980; Whittaker 1988; Schorr, 1988; Chamberlin 1988; McGuire and Shay, 1994; Melton and Barry 1994).

In exploring the value of community wide strategies of family support and prevention of harm, we do not wish to suggest that the major inequalities associated with the conditions in which crime and abuse flourish are unchangeable. Policies which allow deprivation and harm to continue need analysis and challenge. This wider political commitment is closely linked to the project's aim to explore the most effective ways of combating current problems associated with disadvantage. Holman (1988) has argued that social work responses to problems of children and families have traditionally been based on a rescue approach, frequently offered only when family conditions and coping mechanisms are breaking down. To focus only on emergencies and on the responsibilities of parents whilst ignoring the wider context would be to deny the facts amassed over decades. Political action for social and economic change is needed at all levels. However, there is now a body of work which demonstrates that the worst consequences of multiple disadvantages can be lessened by community and family supports (Chamberlin 1988; Miller and Whittaker 1988; Schorr 1988; Gibbons et al. 1990; Gibbons 1992; Zigler and Styfco 1993; Melton and Barry 1994).

Welfare services which are geared to rescue approaches and crisis intervention cannot give adequate attention and emphasis to the supports needed by families. Nor can they draw on the strengths, skills, resources and expertise within communities. We emphasise the value of changing to a more supportive and preventive approach at the same time as urging a commitment by Government agencies to a more realistic approach to the needs of families and neighbourhoods. Planned approaches which facilitate self help initiatives, many of them at relatively low cost, need much greater attention.

Core business of local authorities

In many hard pressed local authorities, the necessary attention to the core business of investigating allegations of abuse and setting up case conferences in child protection swallows up a huge proportion of resources. From some social workers' accounts we estimated that it was not unusual for 40 to 60 hours of professionals' time to go into meetings, interagency liaison, record checks, planning, engaging with judicial processes. All this preparation may take place before a child is seen and well before there can be any assessment of need and offer of support or help to the child or family. Any individual, case by case approach demands huge resources. There would appear to be a bottomless pit of need. Yet the causes of the problems, the conditions associated with them, are untouched by an individualised approach There are questions about the benefit of this huge input of resources to the children concerned and whether the balance of crisis to preventive services is right (Audit Commission 1994; Aldgate and Tunstill 1994; DoH 1995; Parton 1997).

The legal and policy context of family support and preventive work

Section 17 of the Children Act places a duty on the local authority to provide a range and level of services appropriate to meet children's needs and to support families. The regulations and guidance (HMSO 1991 Vol. 2) relating to family support say:

> The Act's emphasis on family support and partnership with parents requires local authorities to adopt a new approach to childcare services. To give family support a high priority in resource allocation may require new thinking across departments on matters such as devolving budget management and accountability.

The United Nations Convention on the Rights of The Child also emphasises the duties of states to provide for children's needs. Yet at a time of economic stringency, very difficult decisions have to be made about what is affordable. Debates about definitions of children in need have been frequent since the Children Act came into effect. There are wide variations in the way local authorities interpret and respond to their responsibilities under this section and many problems associated with a split between protection and welfare (Gibbons (ed.) 1992; Baldwin and Harrison 1993; Aldgate and Tunstill 1994; Parton 1997). Our view following the experience of the Henley Safe Children Project is that children who live in areas of multiple deprivation are at substantial risk of harm and should be identified as 'children in need', or at the very least, Children's Services Plans should be required to address this issue specifically.

Numerous policy and good practice guidelines, interpreting a wide range of legislation, stress the importance of interagency collaboration in promoting the well being of children and families. Working in partnership with consumers, crossing agency boundaries, is emphasised.

The 1990 NHS and Community Care Act requires local authorities and health authorities to work with service users to produce strategic as well as individual plans. The Association of Municipal Authorities' 'Children First' paper identifies:

> The need for a unified, multiagency approach to planning and delivery of services for children with no distinction between education, health, care, leisure, housing and employment.

The white paper 'The Health of The Nation' (DOH 1992) stresses the importance of developing strategies in partnership with the community which can help to reduce 'fear, stigma, or loss of responsibility and choice'.

The 1991 Criminal Justice Act sets out expectations for Social Services and Probation Departments to work together to combat crime and prevent children coming into custody.

All these legislative and policy frameworks acknowledge the multicultural nature of our society, providing the possibility of equal access and rights to services for all citizens, regardless of ethnicity, gender, ability, religion or other social divisions.

The Audit Commission (1994) undertook a study of a number of local authorities and health authorities to consider the extent to which policies and plans are in place to promote 'The well being of children'. This study was based on the view that local authorities have a duty under current legislation to investigate and plan to meet the needs of young children in their areas through advice, counselling, day care and family centres. Their report 'Seen but not heard' (1994) claims that

> Authorities have yet to make the break from providing support dominated by a set range of services to an approach that is needs led.

The Henley Project was set up to contribute to the debate about how the lives of children generally could be enhanced, how risks of abuse could be lessened and the drain on acute and emergency services stemmed. It aimed to encourage the development of strategies, based on detailed local knowledge, which included parents' views, and worked in partnership with them. It drew on a number of findings which suggested that primary prevention of harm to children is possible when planned neighbourhood strategies, fully involving parents, are in place.

Programmes which have been successful in reducing harm to children

A number of projects in the United States and in this country have attempted to take account of environmental stresses and disadvantages in developing preventive programmes. Some have been able to demonstrate that strategies of community support and involvement can reduce:
- child abuse
- crime
- low birth weight
- teenage pregnancies

A wide scale evaluation of projects in the United States (Schorr 1988) describes comprehensive, coordinated services of easily accessible prenatal care in California, Baltimore and Maryland which had reduced numbers of low birth weight babies. Intensive family support programmes in Michigan, Massachusetts and New York are also described which succeeded in reducing child abuse and other forms of family dysfunction, incidence of early school failure, adolescent pregnancy and later school dropout.

Chamberlin (1988) describes a number of community based programmes which have been associated with reductions in low birth weight, child abuse, adolescent pregnancy, school failure and dropout. Detailed accounts are given of an Addison County project and the Ounce Of Prevention Project.

Addison County Parent Child Centre

The Centre was established around 1978 in the largest town in this rural county (population 7,800), with the broad aim of increasing self esteem and communication skills of both parents and children and developing a sense of community. Educational resources and communal washing facilities are available as well as support groups to help people through stressful life situations (first-time parenting, separation/divorce; single parenting). The Centre also provides childcare programmes and co-ordinates various state agencies with the aim of assisting access to services. Because of the rural nature of the area and the isolation of many families it organises a number of outreach activities. Community participation in the running and management of the Centre is an essential feature. The Centre is funded by joint public and private funds and by fundraising activities.

The effects in the county, which may be attributable at least in part to the project, are as follows:

Effects associated with Addison County Project

- A fall in teenage pregnancies: 70/1000 in 1979 – 45/1000 in 1986
- Of those teenagers becoming pregnant:
  90% received antenatal care compared with 49% in the rest of the State;
  1% had low birth weight infant cf. 8.9% in rest of the State
  Infant mortality rate (IMR) 5.6/1000 cf. 11.6/1000 in the rest of the State.
- Amongst families served by the centre:
  welfare dependency fell from 40% in 1983 to 17% in 1987;
  child abuse incidence fell from 21% to 2%;
  only 4 families had a child placed in permanent care;
  adolescent parents receiving high school diploma increased from 30% to 71%.
  (Chamberlin 1988)

Chamberlin describes another project based on the same principles of community involvement, shared funding and community wide services rather than targeting individuals and families identified as high risk.

'Ounce of Prevention' Programme

Aims:

1) empowerment of low income communities through the development of comprehensive family support programmes.
2) prevent family dysfunction.
3) protect healthy coping strategies.
4) promote the optimal development of children and families.

Main services developed:

1) Parent group services — providing emotional support to young parents using a peer group support model.
2) Home visiting — to reduce isolation of pregnant and parenting mothers, to link families with community resources and to provide home based information and support services.
3) Developmental children's services — day care provision, part-time playgroups, mother-child interaction groups, recreation groups for parents and young children etc.
4) Other family support services — broad 'catch-all' category filling gaps in services which are unfunded or inadequate.
5) Primary prevention of unwanted pregnancy — not just based on individual contraception advice but designed to try and address the social pressures underpinning unwanted pregnancy. Attempts to avoid moralising.

The prevention of unwanted pregnancy links to debates in this country about the role of sex education in limiting unplanned teenage pregnancies. Countries where strong emphasis is given to sex education and access to contraceptives — for example Sweden and the Netherlands — have fewer teenage pregnancies (Hudson and Ineichen 1991). Recent cuts in availability of family planning services and unwillingness of some government ministers to ensure that they are readily available to young people are particular problems in the UK.

Preschool programmes

In reviewing the effectiveness of preschool programmes in areas of disadvantage, Zigler and Styfco (1993) argue:

> After a quarter of a century of experimenting with methods of early childhood intervention, it is certainly true that we do not need any more experiments... we can write a coherent federal policy and mount an effective and comprehensive multiyear intervention that will benefit children and families today and for generations to come. (p.xiii)

They review the outcomes of the Head Start and associated programmes in the USA, concluding that programmes which consider the whole child and her or his developmental needs over time, paying attention to parents' needs for support and opportunities and to environmental factors, programmes where there is full parental involvement, are the successful ones. They argue for comprehensive, integrated programmes, over substantial periods of time. Sinclair (1997) draws attention to the advantages to children over time of the High Scope preschool programmes.

Similarly, Veit-Wilson (1993 p.65), considering social disadvantage and child health in Britain claims:

> 'Social disadvantage' means exclusion from society's conventional lifestyle and experiences.... We do not need even more facts about social exclusion. What is required is purposive action.

Reviewing research findings related to the education of under fives in Britain and elsewhere, Clark (1988) stresses the need for continuity of maintenance and support after children have started school. She stresses the links between health, welfare and educational provision, arguing the need for strategic planning across professional boundaries. Like Zigler and Styfco she points to the importance of parental involvement in effective programmes, and emphasises the role of training for parents who can then support others.

An inquiry into the death of Lisa Steele, a young child in Cumbria, recommended a joint policy on preventive services across health and local authority departments (Community Care 9.12.93) Lisa's mother was found guilty of her 'manslaughter'. Her request for a nursery place to support her in coping had been turned down. This joint approach is recommended by the Audit Commission (1994), and built into the requirements of Children's Services Plans.

Social support programmes

In a review of social support programmes in the USA, Miller and Whittaker (1988) suggest that it is the existence of a range of accessible services which is important to success. Similarly, in a review of family centres in England, Gibbons et al. (1990) claim that family relationships and coping mechanisms were enhanced by community support programmes. Parents in the study who described most improvements in family situations were not the ones receiving most help from Social Services Departments but those receiving a variety of help, particularly in day to day care, in an area where there were many local sources of family support. This echoes an earlier finding of Garbarino and Sherman (1980) that the existence of accessible support networks provided a protective influence against child abuse in severely disadvantaged neighbourhoods.

Miller and Whittaker (1988) describe family support programmes ranging from prenatal support by health professionals, through peer support, home aides, day care, parent support groups, parent education. Roberts et al. (1996) review randomised controlled trials of home visiting schemes including some of those described by Miller and Whittaker, mainly those using non professional home visitors. They conclude that there is evidence of effectiveness in reducing injuries to children. Olds (1996) reviewed the effectiveness of two home visiting schemes, to 439 families (200 new families; 239 considered to be at high risk of child maltreatment). Volunteers and paraprofessionals from the same areas as clients visited families. Findings suggest that they were able to reach out effectively — particularly through shared experiences — at times of stress. Coping strategies of mothers improved and the rate of referrals for child maltreatment were substantially below what would have been expected in the population. Volunteers and parents indicated satisfaction. Three main areas of improvement were identified: social support, confidence as a parent and 'affective relationship' with the child.

First Parent Visiting

As a result of the Bristol Child Development Study (Barker 1987), a number of health authorities have trained Health Visitors and volunteers to offer supportive visiting and empower parents in areas of high social stress. Evaluations of the programmes show:
• greater satisfaction with parent/child relationships.
• children more alert and cooperative.
• increased cooperation with increased access to families.
• reductions in cot deaths, hospitalisation, child abuse.

A similar programme in Washington State, USA, for mothers of newborn children, provided by nursing and mental health professionals, showed the following changes:
• increases in social support
• increased use of community resources
• greater satisfaction with social networks and life events (Barnard et al. 1989)

F.A.S.T.

The Families And Schools Together Programme (F.A.S.T.) (McDonald and Billingham, 1990), offered school based family support in many areas of Wisconsin, USA. It started in Madison, and was later accepted as a state wide programme, supported through public funds. It is a preventive programme for children aged 6 – 9 thought to be at risk of future problems because of current behaviour, attainments, apathy or depression in school. Families referred to the programme are under stress and socially isolated, living on benefits, most are single mothers, some suffer depression, many are substance or alcohol abusers.

All are invited as whole families to join the programme — all are volunteers. They agree to attend eight weeks of family group meetings, which are accompanied by outreach work.

The programme attempts to provide intensive support for families and for individual children, whilst taking account of immediate and future practical demands, such as childcare. Trained workers work with parents (usually mothers), both as individuals and in their parental role, trying to increase the quality of interactions and the rewards for positive parenting.

Families are recruited in their homes, often by a F.A.S.T. graduate. They are picked up from their homes and driven to meetings. A free meal is provided for the whole family at the meeting. Childcare is provided for infants and toddlers.

There are monthly meetings — for whole families who have graduated — for the next two years. These include meals, curriculum reviews, and outings; free babysitting is provided to families who attend.

The programme attempts to avoid stigma. F.A.S.T. supports parents while engaging active, voluntary participation in all levels of the programme — deciding future work, recruiting new families, running meetings, fund raising. Some parents go on to become paid staff.

It has a partnership model, with parents and professionals, collaborating with other health and welfare agencies. It develops parent support networks through individual 'buddies' and groups. Evaluations have shown:

increases in:	• self esteem
	• family closeness and support networks
	• attention span at school
improvements in:	• classroom behaviour
	• parent child interactions

Parents consulted in the evaluation believed it helped them to enjoy time with children, get closer to them, understand them better, deal with school problems more effectively.

Newpin

One of the foremost UK preventive programmes is that of Newpin, which has been described as successful in keeping families together. It claims that there were no serious incidents of child abuse amongst families involved in the project during more than ten years of operation (Cox et al., 1992). Newpin offers a supportive service to parents with a variety of problems; welcoming anyone who has a child and feels they need support around:

- feelings of depression — an inability to cope with the business of being a parent;
- being isolated, cut off from family or friends, with no-one to turn to;
- feeling emotionally insecure, unable to trust others;
- unintentionally hurting their children;
- facing difficulties with raising children;
- having lost their sense of identity since becoming parents;
- believing they have no worth or value as people.

A strong emphasis is on training parents in child development and child-care and involvement and training to support other parents and maintain the work of Newpin. Mothers in the greatest adversity were most likely to continue with the programme. They showed striking improvements in self esteem and control over their lives.

Wolfe (1993) like Schorr (1988) and Chamberlin (1988) stresses the importance of developing intervention and preventive programmes which recognise

> that child maltreatment is the product of the interaction between the parent's abilities and resources and the child's emerging behavioural and emotional characteristics.

He reviews programmes taking account of this perspective which also stress problems related to the family context, and the needs of parents and children, rather than focusing only on individual psychopathology. He highlights the connection between maltreatment, poor social and educational development, and behaviour problems in older children. He argues that preventive programmes based on the 'principle of providing the least intrusive, earliest intervention possible' can be beneficial in a number of ways. He reviews family support programmes which have shown improvements in

- parenting knowledge and attitudes
- parent child interactions
- disciplinary behaviour
- reduced reports of maltreatment.

The most successful programmes are those which provide personalised approaches. Wolfe argues, like Zigler and Styfco (1993), that there is persuasive, if initial, evidence to suggest that multilevel programmes which offer additional services as parents require them over a longer period of time are worth the additional expense, compared to less intensive services.

Wolfe also advocates primary prevention programmes, aimed to prevent child abuse, which focus on adolescents. Such programmes would focus on increasing social competence, encouraging greater involvement of males in 'family related issues', 'identifying personal strengths and resources to prepare for present and future roles'. Wolfe

(1991 and 1993) refers to fifteen preventive programmes in Canada and North America based on community and family support. They worked with new and expectant parents, adolescent parents, young people who have been abused, in disadvantaged areas. As well as support, they offered improved access to medical services, parental education groups, consciousness raising activities around aggression, sexual abuse and rape. Parents involved with the programmes felt less stress, their home environments improved, behaviour, play and interaction with their children improved and abuse referrals dropped. They expressed satisfaction with assistance and support when it was non-stigmatising.

Crime prevention

Many of the neighbourhood disadvantages associated with child abuse are also associated with high rates of offences by young people.

Benyon (1993) discusses the links between urban unrest and deprivation, unemployment, racial disadvantage and political exclusion. He argues that these conditions

> result in frustrated expectations, cumulative disappointment and increasing resentment ... reduce identity with mainstream society ... erode social controls and value consensus.

Males particularly are likely to be convicted of criminal and public order offences, yet local women involved with the Henley project claimed that the imbalance in numbers of male and female offenders did not necessarily give an accurate picture of the behaviour which they observed in their neighbourhood. Women on the Steering Group observed that some young women had a role in encouraging street troubles which caused them much concern in the neighbourhood — vandalism, abusive and rowdy behaviour, drugs. Issues of gender are nevertheless crucial to an understanding of how to develop preventive strategies in neighbourhoods, if the overall pattern of offences is taken account of. The large majority of criminal offences are committed by males. In sexual offences the proportion may be as high as 95%. Figures for physical abuse of children suggest that proportions of male and female offenders are about equal (Burchall 1989). This finding obscures, however, the very different amounts of time women spend in childcare compared with men.

Taking up the theme of connections between delinquency and low socioeconomic status and other family problems associated with disadvantage, Utting et al. (1992) argue for crime prevention programmes based on family support and measures to reduce antisocial behaviour. They describe studies which have found that supervision in uncrowded circumstances, good parental discipline, effective 'mothering' are protective against juvenile offending. They also describe findings associating preschool aggression and behaviour problems with 'hostile

care in deprived circumstances'. They argue for a 3 tier approach to delinquency prevention.
1) Universal support services for families.
2) Neighbourhood services in areas of social disadvantage and high crime rates.
3) Family preservation/intensive support programmes for individual families.

Their report emphasises the importance of parent training schemes and neighbourhood supports for families, and attempts to engage males more effectively in childcare and family responsibilities. These approaches, which much of the available evidence supports, were emphasised throughout the Henley Project.

Some of the detail of the report by Utting et al. is however problematic, in that prescriptions do not always match the overall picture. Utting (1995) and Farrington (1996) draw links between social and situational factors and crime, and stress the value of community mobilisation. Yet detailed prescriptions which they advocate focus largely on behaviour in individual families. In practice this can pinpoint *mothers* as responsible for problems, without emphasising sufficiently social and cultural influences on the behaviour of young people and of parents, particularly wider aspects of male behaviour, roles and responsibilities. We would have a similar concern about the focus of Gaudin (1993) in his discussion of effective intervention in cases of neglect.

The cycles of disadvantage studies (Brown and Madge 1982) challenged ideas that personal factors should be the main focus of intervention in improving social behaviour. Problems in behaviour were shown to be linked to continuities of a harmful environment more than personal characteristics. In their report, Utting et al. refer to findings which show that high density of children in a neighbourhood is invariably associated with vandalism. The report cites research showing that the likelihood of boys being involved in crime was eight times higher for those who had friends who committed offences, whatever the level of supervision exercised by the parents. Correlates of family and individual behaviour with criminal acts need to be looked at in relation to cultural and environmental influences and lack of opportunities in disadvantaged neighbourhoods (Farrington and West 1977; 1990; Farrington 1996). These findings, allied to those discussed earlier in the chapter, suggest the need for recognition of the strength of peer influence and the neighbourhood specificity of much juvenile crime.

Attention to neighbourhood and environmental influences is crucial to all childcare and crime prevention initiatives (Sinclair et al. 1997). A community development approach — outreach work with children and young people, neighbourhood campaigns with groups of young people and parents, educational and employment opportunities — needs equal emphasis with family based support and targeted intensive, therapeutic work. An emphasis on partnership with young people and with parents

(Schorr 1988; Chamberlin 1988; Zigler and Styfco 1993; Sinclair et al. 1997) is also important if the alienating and destructive influences of disadvantage are to be lessened.

The common elements of successful programmes

In her account of a large number of evaluations of successful projects, Schorr (1988) identified a number of characteristics which were common. These included:

- comprehensiveness: offering a broad spectrum of services: social, emotional, health care and practical help
- intensiveness
- family and community oriented
- staff with time and skills to develop relationships of trust, respect, collaboration
- continuity of a small committed team
- support from their organisations to be flexible and cross bureaucratic boundaries.

The shape of the services came from the needs they served rather than the precepts and service orientation of professional agencies and their bureaucratic boundaries. *They recognised that needs are untidy*.

This recognition is crucial at a time when changes in health and welfare services in the UK have increasingly pushed towards 'output' led, targeted services, with tight definitions of need and narrow objectives. These are often based on a market philosophy, of what constitutes quality of outcome (Benington 1993). The split into purchaser and provider services does not easily lend itself to a comprehensive, holistic approach to experience and need.

The successful programmes were based on a partnership model, not just of professionals from statutory and voluntary sectors, but with users. They focused on the child in the context of the family, and the family in its surroundings. There was an emphasis on providing services to parents which would help them to make use of services for their children.

Chamberlin (1988) and Zigler and Styfco (1993) stressed the same characteristics. Chamberlin also stressed the importance of long time scales and a clear strategy to take account of community values and accepted principles. He argued that it is important to concentrate on parents' strengths and skills at the same time as being child friendly and concerned to promote children's rights. From the evaluations of successful programmes he concluded that preventive strategies work best when they are concentrated on defined geographical areas where there are substantial numbers of people in a middle range of social and economic disadvantage. Support for children and families in such areas can effectively focus on strengthening community supports which will prevent families becoming overburdened by pressures and sliding into high need. Parallel attention to the small minority of families with very severe problems, intensive, planned, targeted will, of course, still be necessary.

There are many reasons why these approaches need great care, as they could be used to build up profiles of individuals who would then be deemed to be high risk, with consequent stigma and further stress for families. Programmes discussed in this chapter will have encountered this problem. Predicting accurately those families where abuse, crime, mental health problems are likely is fraught with methodological problems and ethical dilemmas. For every case predicted accurately, there are likely to be many predicted wrongly. The causative pathways to such behaviours and problems are complex, and definitions are imprecise (Gelles 1982; Starr 1982; Montgomery 1982; Parton 1985; Baldwin and Spencer 1993). Labelling individuals may make the problems more rather than less likely. Chamberlin (1988) argues persuasively that community wide strategies can avoid these problems, by focusing collective attention on need and responsibility for improving the conditions locally. Thompson (1994) explores some of the complexities of developing social supports. Sinclair (1997) stresses the importance of open access, self help and mutuality and the avoidance of stigma.

The complexity of the situations involved, the enormous number of variables, problems with research methodologies, mean that claims about the effectiveness of particular preventive strategies will always need to be treated with caution. (Gough (1993); Baldwin and Spencer (1993); Macdonald and Roberts (1995)). Yet a great deal is known about the conditions in which children thrive and the conditions in which harm is likely. Strategies which aim to maximise healthful, life enhancing environments, are justified by demographic and epidemiological statistics, as well as moral values.

Principles

A commitment to try to encourage and facilitate the development of supports and resources needed for health and social wellbeing has been one of the key principles in the Henley Project. A second principle has been that of partnership with parents, stressed as an essential factor in successful programmes. Such partnership cannot be based on token consultation or involvement. It depends on structures of planning and decision making which involve users of services throughout the process. Power differentials and conflicts of interest have to be dealt with by all concerned. Commitment to equal opportunities, involving fully minority groups and groups with special needs, is involved. Attention is needed to communicating effectively the constraints on decisions, ensuring access to information in minority community languages, free from professional jargon. Arrangements for meetings, consultations and involvement which take account of practical demands such as childcare are important. Equal attention to the processes of work and the styles of relationships as to aims and structures underpins this partnership approach.

Issues

In drawing attention to the wider context of child abuse and some of the links between disadvantage and harm to children, we want to take care not to stereotype and further stigmatise disadvantaged groups. Most families provide healthy and loving environments, often in difficult circumstances. In the Henley Project we have tried to acknowledge and build on the strengths and skills of many varied groups. We are conscious, however, that our work has taken place in a largely white neighbourhood. It cannot adequately represent the experience and views of Black groups. Yet we need to learn from their experience. Some minority ethnic groups, whilst being among the most disadvantaged, have lower than average rates of reported child abuse and crime. Knowledge of their community and family strengths and child rearing patterns is important for preventive strategies (Devore and Sclesinger 1987). We hope that other projects will continue to explore strengths and needs of minority groups, including children of mixed racial heritage. The link between racial harassment and abuse and harm to children needs much further study.

Although the Henley Project set out to work with *parents* it was mainly mothers who involved themselves in the project. This is an unsurprising reflection of the traditional patterns of childcare. Yet it highlights gender as a major issue. Behaviour and responses of males and females, as carers or as individuals, are very different.

As has been stressed, physical abuse of young children is said to be inflicted almost equally by males and females (NSPCC 1987; Burchall 1989), but apparent equality needs to be considered in the light of very different roles and amounts of contact in caring. The most serious cases of harm are more likely to be committed by men (Wolfe 1991).

Sexual offenders are much more frequently male than female — as many as 95% to 5% (Finkelhor 1984; Russell 1986; La Fontaine 1990; Kelly et al. 1992). This applies whether it is abuse of boys or girls. Few females go on to abuse children after being abused themselves, yet it would appear that a significant number of boys do. We need to try to understand the significant dynamics at work here and consider how community wide strategies may take some account of them. We need to avoid any risk of putting yet further burdens on mothers, and consider how men may be encouraged to take more responsibilities in childcare. At a time of mass unemployment there may be creative ways of involving men and women in opportunities for childcare and training, to develop neighbourhood schemes which will enhance the environment for children and for adults.

Loneliness, stress and social isolation of women with young children, are associated with depression (Brown and Harris 1978; Blackburn 1991), health problems and stresses and difficulties for children (Chamberlin 1988; Blaxter 1993; Reading 1997). The attitudes and behaviour of men can be heavily implicated in perpetuating these problems. Community strategies of family support will involve raising consciousness of sexist attitudes, male violence and sexual abuse. Projects to look with men at the implications for children's safety of current male involvement in childcare and socialisation would be illuminating.

A great deal is known in general about the conditions and circumstances in which children thrive and achieve their potential, and those in which they come to harm. The views and opinions of parents and workers in the Henley area of Coventry as they relate their experience to this wider context, will be the subject of the next two chapters.

2 Background to the Henley Safe Children Project

Our aim in this book is to connect the lived, day by day experience of families in a particular neighbourhood with wider knowledge and understandings of children's and families needs.

We hope that by making connections between the general and the particular we can illustrate how analysis and overview may best inform local policy and practices in family support and childcare.

This chapter sets out the background to the Henley Safe Children Project, some of the characteristics of the area and the ways in which information was gathered.

The Henley Safe Children Project was an action research project, initially funded through Home Office Safer Cities and later supported by the NSPCC. It was jointly managed by NSPCC and the University of Warwick.

Before the project was set up, discussions had been held with Social Services, Education, Health, Probation, NSPCC, Save the Children Fund and other voluntary agencies and with groups of residents in the area. The development worker, Lyn Carruthers, was appointed to work with these groups for an initial period of eighteen months, extended for a further twelve months. After the main work of the project she was employed as a permanent member of the Coventry NSPCC team, working with local people and workers to develop preventive strategies which draw on the findings of the project.

The Henley area of Coventry was chosen for the project because at the time of planning it had the highest number of children — overall and proportionally — on the Child Protection Register. A mapping exercise, done by one of the authors for the whole city in 1989, had shown that referrals were clustered in particular districts within the ward .

The area of the project has a largely white population. The mapping had also shown that there was a substantial under representation of South Asian children on the City's Child Protection Register. As South Asian groups form a substantial minority within Coventry, and in some areas make up approximately 50% of the population, funding was sought for a second parallel study to consult South Asian groups about their family support and child protection needs. This project began in 1993 with funding from NSPCC and another charitable trust and from local authorities in the Midlands. It also was jointly managed by NSPCC and the University of Warwick. The main findings are reported in the final report of the Hifazat Surukhia Project (Atkar et al 1997).

We are conscious that there are still other major gaps in information about needs for family support and preventive work in child protection which these two projects cannot hope to fill. For example children of mixed racial heritage were found to be over represented on the Coventry Child Protection Register in the 1989 mapping exercise and are heavily over represented in public childcare systems. Their experience and needs still require greater priority and study. Equally there is need for greater attention to those children and families who may have special needs because of physical or intellectual impairments.

We hope nevertheless that our account of the work of the Henley Safe Children Project — in spite of gaps — will identify issues relevant to research and development work with these and other groups, and be of value to a wide range of people concerned to promote the wellbeing of all children.

The Aims of the Project

The aims agreed by participants and funders were:
- to identify and promote preventive initiatives which aim to reduce levels of concern about child protection within the Henley area;
- to work with parents to define their own needs and problems in bringing up children, identify resources needed and preferred solutions;
- to help parents provide written accounts of their experiences, which can be used in training health and welfare professionals;
- through collaborative work with local people and professionals, to increase awareness of the range of difficulties experienced by parents in deprived neighbourhoods and so improve the sensitivity and effectiveness of local health, education and social services policy and practice;
- to demonstrate the need for and usefulness of self help and family support programmes as a major priority in child protection;
- to work with other professionals and local groups to develop self help groups and other initiatives which aim to improve support for parents.

Characteristics of the Henley Ward

Child protection referrals

When the project was planned, the Henley ward had the highest number of children on the Child Protection Register — overall and proportionally — for any area of the city. During the life of the project this changed slightly, with other areas registering higher proportions from time to time. However referrals remained very high in the Henley Ward throughout. Figure 2 shows the numbers of children registered in March 1989.

Figure 1　Map of Coventry showing March 1989 registrations

Number of children on child protection register
in different wards of Coventry

Crown and ED-LINE copyright

Source: Coventry Social Services Department

Within the Henley ward there was substantial clustering of referrals in particular areas — most particularly in the area known as Wood End, but also in parts of Bell Green and Henley Green. The focus of the project's work was on these areas. Boundaries for health and other services were not coterminous, although efforts were made later to define common boundaries across agencies. The lack of consistent boundaries leads to some difficulties in matching and interpreting data. The information which follows is drawn from national census data, local health authority reports and local authority department reports.

By the time the project began, the area of focus no longer had the highest proportion of child protection referrals, but was still very near the top of the scale. The figures for Wood End and Bell Green in Table 2 cover the project area; they include the figures for Henley Green. The area had the highest rates of children in the care of the local authority at that time.

Table 2 **Children on the Child Protection Register in wards in Coventry; April 1991 (per 1000 children population as from 1981 census boundaries)**

District	No. on Register	Children in Area (0–19)	No. per 1000 children popn.
Hillfields (St. Michael's)	49	4335	11.3
Foleshill	58	6511	8.9
Holbrooks	5	4595	1.1
Radford	12	6221	1.9
Bablake (Coundon)	21	5854	3.6
Allesley	6	5527	1.1
Tile Hill	7	8354	6.8
Canley	27	3037	8.9
Earlsdon	24	4511	5.3
Cheylesmore	11	7865	1.4
Upper Stoke	25	5001	5.0
Stoke Aldermore	29	4313	6.7
Willenhall	33	8203	4.0
Wyken	16	8098	2.0
Bell Green	**32**	**5676**	**5.6**
Wood End	**65**	**6003**	**10.8**
Total	420	94104	4.5

Source: Coventry Social Services Dept; Research and Planning, 1992

The ward is on the edge of the industrial city of Coventry (population 360,000). It has a number of public housing estates within it (accommodating 35.5% of households) as well as more affluent areas of private housing. The housing is mainly low-rise, but there is a large number of blocks of apartments. Only 0.3% of households in the Henley ward are without the sole use of bath or shower and inside W.C. 88.2% of households have central heating. The average household size is 2.7.

Although there are large areas of open space, there are no parks in the area and there is very little safe or supervised play space. The lack of safety on the streets and in open spaces has been a major concern of residents' and parents' groups over many years.

Employment

According to 1991 census data, unemployment for the ward was 14.72%. This figure masks a very high proportion of women — 2070 out of 5570 — who were described as 'economically inactive'. They were not in employment, but were not actively seeking work. More than 40% of the adults in the ward were 'economically inactive'. The national average for unemployment was 7.2%.

In September 1992 the City's Economic Development and Planning Department recorded unemployment of 16.8% for the Henley Ward, compared with 13.5% for the city as a whole. 1991 Census figures showed that in parts of the Wood End area of the ward male unemployment was 50%. In households where there was a lone parent — most usually female — 84% were shown to be 'economically inactive'.

Health

In 1989 local health authority figures showed an average age of death for women in the Henley ward of 67 years — 4 years lower than for any other ward in Coventry. Male and female deaths together over the period 1986-1989 were the earliest age for the city. It was one of the wards with the highest proportion of low birthweight babies for the city. The health clinic serving the part of the ward where substantial clusters of child protection referrals were noted in 1989 and 1992, also showed the highest rates of accidents for children under 5 in the city.

The ward had the highest rate of emergency admissions to hospital for the city during 1990-1991; 29% above average. It also had the highest overall rate of admissions to hospital. Admissions for gynaecological problems were 39% above average. Paediatric admissions were 29% above average and 10% higher than in any other ward in the city. Other more affluent wards had up to 15% below average admissions — so the chances of admission to hospital for Henley children was 44% higher than children in these wards.

The health clinic serving the part of the ward known as Wood End recorded the highest accident rate for children under 5 for the city. The clustering of high accident rates and high child protection referrals corresponds.

Crime

The ward had a very high overall crime rate, but local police figures showed a substantial concentration in the part of the ward where high numbers of childhood accidents had been noted. This section of the ward had the highest crime rate and the highest number of referrals to Juvenile Justice teams for any residential area of the city. It had the highest numbers of burglaries, criminal damage offences and sexual assaults outside the city centre. The figures reported for the Bell Green district were lower than for other districts in the Henley Project area.

Education

The education department would not release figures on truancy and other school absences, because of the stigmatising effect this can have on schools and neighbourhoods. However poor school attendance and under achievement were seen as problems by many of the local workers involved with the project. Two of the secondary schools for the area were in the 3 lowest scoring comprehensive schools in Coventry, for the percentage of 15 year olds achieving 5 or more grades A–C at GCSE, according to nationally published figures (1994 November 22nd, Guardian). One of them was also the school with the lowest percentage of pupils gaining 1 or more grades A–G in GCSE exams.

Indicators of disadvantage

Coventry Health Area statistics showed that Wood End and Bell Green areas were among the most deprived areas of Coventry, where Jarman, Townsend, Carstairs or Z scores were calculated. Henley was one of the city's wards with the highest number of:
- individuals unemployed;
- households without a car;
- households living with more than one person to a room;
- household heads in semi or unskilled occupations;
- households who were not owner occupiers.

Using 1991 Census figures, the City Council calculated how its wards and enumeration districts compared with other districts in the West Midlands region, according to indicators of disadvantage as measured through Z scores. Z scores were calculated according to:
- the numbers of lone parent households;
- over crowding (more than 1 person per room);
- unemployment;
- households with a lone pensioner;
- households lacking basic amenities.

The higher the Z score, the greater the indicators of disadvantage. Nineteen % of Coventry's enumeration districts fell into the lowest 10% for the region. When looking at its proportion of the most disadvantaged districts, this places it as 3rd city in the region. Birmingham, with 28.8% of its districts in the lowest 10%, was first, and Wolverhampton, with 20.68%, second.

**Figure 2   Map showing areas of Coventry falling into the most
disadvantaged 10% for the (West Midlands) region**

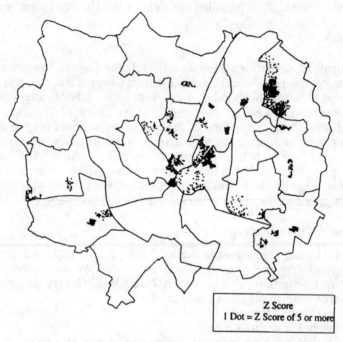

Z Score
1 Dot = Z Score of 5 or more

Crown and ED-LINE copyright

Source: Population Census, 1991

The overall position of the Henley Ward, within which the project
area was situated, was 8th most disadvantaged within the city, out of 18
wards. Its overall Z score was 2.38, whereas the Foleshill and St.
Michael's wards had scores above 6. The average score for the city was
1.75.

However, if we consider the regional placing of the most disadvantaged 10% of enumeration districts, and the wards which contain a high
proportion of these, the picture which emerges is very different. There
were two enumeration districts in the Henley ward with Z scores between
9 and 13, six with scores between 7 and 8.9 and three with scores
between 5 and 6.9. This calculation placed Henley ward as the 3rd most
disadvantaged in the city. Its overall position reflects very substantial differences within the ward — with some enumeration districts having Z
scores reflecting relative affluence and advantage (between minus 5.75
and minus 4).

Two other wards in Coventry showing higher numbers of enumeration districts in the most disadvantaged 10% in the West Midlands region had high proportions of minority ethnic groups. Minority ethnic groups are generally under represented on UK child protection registers.

Links between indicators of disadvantage and child protection referrals

In 1992 we made a detailed map of referrals of cases involving child protection concerns, to the social work teams covering Wood End, Henley Green and Bell Green. There were 218 referrals between October 1991 and December 1992. Of these referrals, 144 were located inside the part of the Henley Ward covered by the project. Figure 5 shows the geographical spread of these referrals. It follows closely the clustering noted in the mapping done in 1989. The referrals which do not appear in this figure were mainly from parts of the Wood End and Bell Green areas which fell outside the Henley Ward: they did not show up in clusters, but were fairly evenly spread. A few referrals had come from other parts of the city.

Because of the commitment to protect the anonymity of families, a method of mapping referrals was chosen which could not guarantee 100% accuracy on the borders of enumeration districts. However, calculations of rates of child protection referrals based on the mapping suggest that E.D.s with Z scores less than the mean had referral rates of about 12 per 1000 compared with up to 56 per 1000 in E.D.s with Z scores greater than the mean.

In those E.D.s with Z scores above the mean which also had the highest rates of referrals, between 35% and 46% of their residents were under 18 years old. On average, 38% of their residents were under 15, almost twice as high as the proportion for Coventry as a whole. There were 3 E.D.s which scored very high on rates of disadvantage, but not on child protection referrals. In these districts fewer than 25% of residents were under 18.

The proportions of cases referred who went through full investigations and case conferences and were placed on the Child Protection Register, mirror those referred to by NSPCC (1994) and Messages from Research (DoH 1995) where only 1 in 7 investigations led to registration. The Audit Commission (1994) found 'up to 2/3 of referrals investigated were dropped before being considered for registration at a case conference'.

Figure 3 Child protection referrals between Oct 91 – Dec 92 for Wood End and Bell Green, falling within the Henley Ward

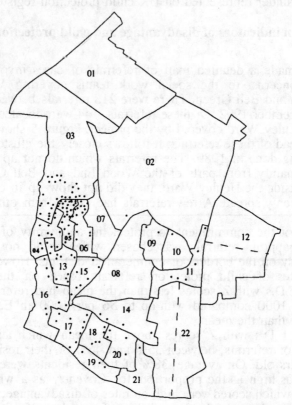

Crown and ED-LINE copyright

Source: Coventry Social Services Department

Each dot represents a household: more than one child was referred in some cases. Some households were referred on more than one occasion. There is a broad correspondence between areas of severe disadvantage and the clusters of child protection referrals. These districts have up to 40% of their population under 18.

In the nine month period monitored for number of referrals reaching the Register in the Henley area, only 14 out of 139 were registered. Some of the 139 were referred more than once. The geographical spread of those placed on the Register follows the same pattern as those of referrals, but the much smaller numbers do not show nearly as starkly as the referral figures the intense level of activity in child protection in the severely disadvantaged districts.

The mapping of child protection referrals between October 1991 and December 1992 showed clustering around the enumeration districts with the highest Z scores. Eight enumeration districts within the cluster stand out as having very high rates of referral — FF 03, 04, 05, 06, 13, 15, 16, 17.

Table 3 shows how these districts compared with others in the ward, in relation to average numbers of people in households, proportions under 18 and percentage unemployed. All these districts had above 15% unemployment. More than 34% of their population were under 18, compared with the national average of 25% (Audit Commission 1994). In some districts unemployment was over 25%; in some there were more than 45% of residents under 18.

When interpreting the Z scores, it needs to be remembered that this is an area of relatively modern housing, with good amenities — so that housing disadvantage and overcrowding do not play a major role in high Z scores.

Parts of enumeration districts 12 and 22 fell outside the area covered by the two teams whose referrals were monitored. Enumeration districts 23 to 32 also fell outside the two areas.

The high concentration of child abuse referrals cannot be accounted for solely by the high proportion of young children in these enumeration districts. Some enumeration districts with over 35% of their population under 18 had many times more referrals than areas with much lower proportions. None of the enumeration districts with fewer than 25% of their population under 18 showed strikingly high referral rates.

A very high proportion of children to adults in an area of severe unemployment and low income, where many health problems are experienced, suggests a level of difficulty and stress within the neighbourhood which would demand exceptional personal resources to handle. Section 17 of the Children Act, setting out the responsibility of local authorities to provide a range of services to support families and children in need is highly relevant in such a neighbourhood. Bebbington and Miles' (1989) study of the characteristics of families of children who come into care documents links between individual and family disadvantages and likelihood of coming into care. It also shows that the rate of entry into care in areas with many poor wards is higher than would be predicted from family related social indicators alone, implying that coming from a poor area has an independent effect on the probability of entry. International

Table 3   Census data by enumeration district — Henley Ward, Coventry

Enumeration District (FF)	Total Persons	Average persons per Household	Under 18 (%)	Unemployed (%)	Z Scores
01	567	2.5	19.6	2.15	-3.03
02	558	2.6	19.2	4.85	-0.70
03	**404**	**2.5**	**35.4**	**16.67**	**6.77**
04	**623**	**3.0**	**39.5**	**26.21**	**7.28**
05	**569**	**3.0**	**45.7**	**15.38**	**8.56**
06	**563**	**2.7**	**40.1**	**20.00**	**8.51**
07	357	1.9	23.2	7.83	2.88
08	462	2.8	23.8	4.20	-4.12
09	588	2.9	26.7	4.46	-1.84
10	560	3.0	25.9	6.69	-0.90
11	499	2.7	24.0	3.28	-0.01
12	644	2.6	22.8	11.11	2.91
13	**539**	**3.2**	**46.2**	**24.22**	**9.20**
14	457	2.2	26.7	14.86	5.78
15	**661**	**2.9**	**43.0**	**20.50**	**7.75**
16	**425**	**2.5**	**34.8**	**29.94**	**7.22**
17	**571**	**2.9**	**35.7**	**15.05**	**5.59**
18	**552**	**3.0**	**43.7**	**26.83**	**8.22**
19	429	2.1	33.1	18.05	6.79
20	432	2.2	21.1	22.44	9.12
21	481	2.2	22.5	10.90	4.86
22	648	2.9	11.0	7.33	3.72

Source: Population Census, 1991

Z scores 0 = average score; the higher the score, the more disadvantaged the district.

figures for child protection registrations consistently demonstrate correlations between poverty and registrations (Creighton and Noyes 1990; Sedlak 1993).

A small proportion of adults bringing up large numbers of children in such an environment will have exceptional demands made on them in attempting to keep their children safe, healthy and socially responsible.

Minority ethnic groups

Census figures from 1981 showed that 3.8% of people in the Henley ward were from minority ethnic groups. City of Coventry Social Services Trends for 1990 established, from the Census figures for 1981, that 7.25% of households in the Wood End and Bell Green areas of the ward had a 'head of household' from the New Commonwealth or Pakistan.

Accurate figures for the percentage of childcare cases from these households were not available. However, in the 1990 Trends, the number of Asian and Caribbean households on the case loads of these district teams was 17 out of 819. Proportionally, 58 would have been expected, if there had been no major change in area composition since the 1981 Census. A further 17 cases were registered as of 'mixed parentage'. A number of these could fall into the category described under 'head of household from New Commonwealth or Pakistan'. However, even if all of them did, this would still leave a substantial under representation of these groups having access to Social Services. A number of workers involved with the Henley Safe Children Project said that these groups were more likely to seek help from city wide services, which offer specialist services to minority groups, than from local services. The project development worker worked with these city wide groups to try to make contact with minority groups living in the Henley ward who would be willing to talk to her about their experiences in the area.

1991 Census figures showed a proportion of 'white' residents in the Henley ward of 94.2%, and 'non-white' 5.8%. In some enumeration districts the percentage of 'nonwhite' residents was as low as 1.4%. In the enumeration districts which were the focus of the project the proportion of 'nonwhite' residents varied between 1.4% and 13.6%.

It is not possible to make accurate comparisons between data from the 1981 and 1991 censuses in relation to ethnicity. In the 1981 census families were asked to say if the household head was from the New Commonwealth or Pakistan. The relevance of such a question changes over time, as more citizens whose families come from these areas will themselves have been born in Britain. Table 4 uses the classifications of the 1991 census to show the ethnic groups of residents in the Henley Ward.

Table 4 Ethnic groups of residents – Henley Ward

	Total	%
White	17030	94.2
Black Caribbean	250	1.4
Black African	20	0.1
Black Other	140	0.8
Indian	410	2.3
Pakistani	10	–
Bangladeshi	3	–
Chinese	30	0.2
Other	190	1.1
Persons born in Republic of Ireland	840	n/a

Source: Population Census, 1991

Resources available to the area

The statistics set out so far present a worrying picture of problems and stresses for local residents, particularly for parents attempting to bring up children.

Yet the Wood End and Bell Green areas had had substantial attention and resources made available to them. There had been a major programme of refurbishment for housing stock which was built in the 1950s — to alleviate problems of damp, heating and maintenance. Numerous projects, including outreach, community safety and employment initiatives, community education and youth work were active in the area. Schools and nurseries in the area attempted to provide good models of multicultural education, of cooperation and family support; health and Social Services were active in developing responsive neighbourhood services in spite of major financial constraints. Numerous groups were seeking to improve interagency cooperation and to increase family support.

Soon after the Henley Safe Children Project began, the local authority set up an Area Management Team to coordinate services and to take initiatives in liaison and collaboration with local residents and groups. At the same time a family project was opened in the area, in a new specially designed building, funded by the Urban Programme. A development worker, employed by Save the Children Fund, worked from the project to develop local initiatives in family and neighbourhood support and information and practical help and access to a wide range of services. The work of the Henley Safe Children Project was developed very closely with groups involved with the Area Management Team and the Family Project.

Childcare services

Following the implementation of the Children Act, the Social Services Department set up an Under 8s Forum, chaired by the Social Services Group Manager for under 5s. This group, with the Area Management Team, initiated a review of resources for children, and sought views of local people about childcare needs and problems. The information which was gained following the initiative provides a picture of the resources available to parents, as well as showing different levels of access and of satisfaction. There were difficulties in gaining access to Black parents views — it took the whole length of the project for us to feel satisfied that we had an adequate picture. Some detail of parents' — mainly mothers' — views has been included in this section because it seems crucial to consider supports for childcare alongside other characteristics of the area. External supports and easy access to childcare may be crucial priorities in an area where there are many pressures and many hindrances to safe childrearing.

Questionnaires for local parents had been agreed soon after the Henley Project began. The Henley development worker was involved in supervising the local outreach workers who were engaged to do the fieldwork. 133 people were interviewed. A summary of some of their replies is given in Table 5.

Survey staff said that they had been unsuccessful in involving Black people in the survey, and a subgroup of the Under 5s Forum was set up to look at Black Access to Child Care Services (B.A.C.C.S.). In the original survey, 20 African Caribbean families had been approached, but had not wished to be involved.

The B.A.C.C.S group consisted of two workers with a good knowledge of the local area (the Henley worker and a community education worker), a social work student with experience of working with African Caribbean families and a worker with language skills and experience of working with Asian families. All the subgroup were women: two white, one African Caribbean and one Asian worker.

The Henley Project Worker was much more heavily involved in carrying out the B.A.C.C.S. Survey than the original survey. She was involved in the funding proposal, advertising, interviewing and recruiting the outreach workers, as well as their supervision. She was also involved in organising a group session for parents involved in the survey, and the presentation of findings to local agencies. She was responsible for writing the first draft of the B.A.C.C.S. Report. The work took place over the year March 1993–March 1994.

Table 5   Use of local childcare services (131 respondents)

Resource (no. using resource)	Comments of those interviewed
Baby clinic (103)	55 – met children's needs 55 – held at convenient times 8 – sometimes had long wait staff told them 'how to do it' not always open when needed milk
Nursery (86)	too expensive no places for children below normal age range more provision needed for children to stay all day
Parents and toddlers groups (48)	at inconvenient times didn't know where to find hard to get involved
Playgroups (53)	expensive not enough places
Babysitters (28)	no–one to ask unsure who could be trusted
Creches (27)	don't know where to find staff aren't always qualified children not always happy there too far away too expensive
Holiday playschemes (26)	opening hours inconvenient expensive
Childminders (10)	too expensive
After school care (1)	unaware of any provision

Source: Coventry Social Services Department

Twenty-nine of those interviewed said they had had to turn down work because of childcare problems. Thirteen had had to turn down education or training.

Other times when the need for childcare was not met were identified as:

• school holidays; after school; evenings.
• 33 said their childcare needs were not met during holidays.

Situations identified where there was a need for help with childcare included:
• birth of a baby; shopping; hospital appointments

Eighty of those interviewed identified a need for a park or play area as the single resource which they would most like to have in the area.

Fourteen of those interviewed would have welcomed the opportunity for training to develop their interest in working with Under 5s.

Table 6   Use of local services for Black children (66 respondents)

Resource (no. using resource)	Comments of those interviewed
Baby clinic (37)	21 – met children's needs 20 – held at convenient times 2 – had language problems 1 – no welcome for Black people 1 – times not convenient
Nursery (40)	11 – met children's needs prefer longer hours access was restrictive
Parents and Toddlers Groups (8)	4 – met children's needs not used by African Caribbean parents or parents of children of mixed African Caribbean heritage child wouldn't go expensive time wasting none in area lack of information
Playgroups (16)	not long enough hours too far away
Babysitters (5)	no comment
Creches (7)	too expensive unsure where to find
Holiday playschemes (3)	no comment
Childminders (3)	too expensive 1 – difficulty finding minder for disabled child
After school care (3)	no comment

Source: BACCS

Of the sixty six parents involved in the survey, there were:
• 12 African Caribbean parents
• 1 African parent
• 44 Asian parents
• 9 parents of children of mixed heritage (2 mixed heritage Asian, 7 mixed heritage African Caribbean).

Four of those interviewed said that they had had to turn down work because of childcare problems. Eleven had had to turn down education or training. Other times when the need for childcare was not met were identified as:
• after school;
• summer holidays;

The lack of facilities for Muslim children was highlighted.

Situations identified where there was a need for help with childcare included:
• during the day — for a break;
• not being able to get out of the house on your own;
• help with a disabled child with behavioural problems;
• shopping;
• difficulties of travelling with young children.

Thirty-eight of those interviewed identified a need for more childcare provision as the single resource which they would most like to have in the area. Twenty-four said they wanted a safe play area, or park.

Comparisons were made between the original survey of white parents and the B.A.C.C.S. Survey of Black parents.

Proportionally twice as many Black parents as white had not used a childcare service. Apart from nursery provision, a significantly lower number of Black parents used all childcare services.

No African Caribbean parents or parents of children of mixed heritage (African Caribbean) used parents and toddlers groups.

Table 7   Proportion using childcare services

Resource	White Parents	Black Parents
Baby clinic	just under 80%	just over 50%
Nursery	just under 67%	nearly 67%
Parents & toddlers groups	just over 33%	about 10%
Playgroup	just over 33%	nearly 25%

Source: BACCS

Proportionally the same numbers of white and Black parents were on waiting lists for nurseries. Half as many Black parents as white parents were on playgroup waiting lists and none were on holiday play schemes lists.

Twelve % of Black parents had been turned down for a childcare service as opposed to 6% of white parents. Twenty-five % approximately (8 out of 30) of Black parents had never asked about a childcare service, whereas only 5% approximately (4 out of 98) white parents had never asked.

Equal proportions of Black and white parents had turned down education and training opportunities; slightly more Black than white parents had turned down work.

Roughly equal proportions of parents said that they would like to work if their childcare needs were met, however 30% of Black parents compared with approximately 18% of white parents said they would like to study or train.

A higher proportion of Black parents said they were interested in working with under 5s: 23% compared with 14.8% of white parents. Half of the Black parents who stated they were interested in working with under 5s said they already had some involvement with providing under 5s services.

Eighty % of white parents said they wanted a safe play area or park compared with 36% of Black parents. Fifty-seven point five % of Black parents said they wanted more childcare facilities compared with 25% of white parents.

There were three main issues mentioned by Black parents which were not mentioned by white parents: language barriers — wanting English classes; lack of facilities for Asian families and racism — particularly racial harassment of their children.

Issues in making contact with and listening to Black families

There were key differences about the process of making contact with Black parents compared with white parents. The B.A.C.C.S. work needed a much greater time commitment than the original survey. New contacts needed to be established with Black organisations, the majority of which were city wide, without a base in the local area. These new contacts needed to be established before recruitment of the outreach workers and making contact with local Black parents. This meant identifying appropriate Black organisations and seeing that they were recognised as local service providers.

Once the outreach workers were in post they used organisations outside the area who worked with Black families to make contact with people. The most effective responses were from a voluntary sector education and training project and from religious centres. The electoral register was used to establish where Asian families lived and contact was made by knocking on doors. Personal contacts of the outreach workers who lived in the area were approached, and provided introductions.

This contrasted with the experience of the original survey where a substantial number of questionnaires were distributed through established networks and groups.

The B.A.C.C.S. outreach workers outlined some key issues in making contact with Black parents. They found that Black families did not want to talk to white people who were seen as officials of the council. Time was needed to build up trust with groups before people were willing to cooperate. The outreach workers discovered that Black families had little information about services Because they believed they should and did treat everyone the same, some professionals showed reservations about cooperating in a survey of Black people. These issues are explored more fully in Chapter 5.

Under use of childcare resources

The surveys showed under use of some childcare provision, even though there were parents who felt they needed more opportunities to leave their children, particularly for education, training and work. Help during school holidays, help to enable parents to keep hospital appointments and to go shopping were identified as needs which were not met.

In February 1992, 73 places were registered with childminders in the area compared with 129 in Wyken, 147 in Walsgrave and 177 in Coundon — all more affluent wards of the city. At the time of the childcare survey, there were 85 places registered, of which only 46 were being used.

Henley is an area where two thirds of families are on low incomes: either in receipt of housing benefits or entirely dependent on state benefits, so affording paid childcare presents a major problem. Childminding, which could be seen as a potential support service for many families with young children, but which is relatively costly to users, is less used than in most areas of the city.

In 1993 a survey was done of the views of a city wide women's development network about the effect of the Children Act on their childcare provision. Forty-three members responded. This survey showed that there were major concerns that the amount of childcare provision would be reduced. Creches were seen as particularly vulnerable because of more demanding expectations following the Act. Respondents believed that the effects would be felt most heavily in areas characterised by disadvantage.

Issues of childcare and protection

The facts and figures on health in the Henley area alongside low income, pockets of very high unemployment and high levels of crime and danger on the streets, give some indication of the difficulties parents face in bringing up their children in health and safety. The burden of care, responsibility and guidance on the relatively small proportion of adults in the neighbourhood is enormous. It is a burden which traditional responsibilities and the experience from this and other projects suggest falls most heavily on mothers.

This is the context in which high child protection referrals and childhood accidents have to be understood. It raises questions about the range of resources which are needed by families, to bring up their children safely, in the presence of deprivation and major stresses, in an area where there are numerous harmful and antisocial influences on them and on their children. At a time when increasing attention was being paid to the failings of parents, increasing the pressures on them whilst not necessarily giving any practical help to achieve the high standards they themselves want for their children, those involved with the Henley Project wanted to document the views of parents about their successes, their needs and their concerns. Skilled parenting was seen as crucial; but so was the economic and social environment in which it took place.

We set out :

to investigate
- parents' methods of keeping children safe;
- major sources of stress in bringing up children;
- their views of family and community supports needed to prevent harm to children;
- ways they could help and support each other.

to encourage
- an effective flow of information between parents and workers;
- shift in priorities to preventive strategies, away from concentration of resources in crisis work and investigations of abuse;
- participation by local parents and residents in neighbourhood planning.

Equally, we were committed to listening to the views and priorities of local people, adapting our aims and assumptions in the light of theirs.

The work of the project

During the first four months of the project the development worker visited about 40 agencies and key individuals in the area to give information about the Henley Project and build up a knowledge of the area and the services being provided. This work was seen as an essential preparation for meeting parents to discuss with them their views of child-care needs and safety issues. She also made contact with a city wide agency — OSABA — for African Caribbean women and children.

After this preparation work a further four months were spent making contact with groups and individuals who might be interested in joining the Project Steering Group, joining in other work with the project or simply giving their views. Leaflets publicising the aims of the project and inviting local people to give their views or participate in activities were widely distributed. Strong emphasis was given in the leaflets to the paramount aim being to protect and promote the wellbeing of children, so confidentiality was only assured as long as it was compatible with such an aim. Pilot sessions were run with individuals and groups about their experiences of bringing up children in the area. The development worker's involvement in collecting information about childcare services in the area following the implementation of the Children Act has already been described.

At the end of this period a Steering Group was set up with the aim of advising the project worker, providing a forum for the exchange of views between local people and health, education and welfare agencies, as well as disseminating the findings of the project throughout its life.

Premises for meeting parents and workers were identified, close to the main focus area for the study. Creche and other childcare arrangements were made. Close working links were established with workers and groups in a Community Education Project and Family Project.

For seven months there was intensive consultation with individuals and groups, documenting their views of childcare needs and issues, their experiences as parents and residents and their views and experiences of childcare services. Some of these groups came together only to document their views, others continued as activity and support groups. With the local Family Project worker the development worker also set up a 'Drop In' for local people at a newly opened centre. Between 8 and 10 parents regularly attended the 'Drop In', sharing their views about a wide range of topics and concerns about bringing up children in the area.

Contact with the Black women's citywide group OSABA continued with the aim of documenting views of Black parents at a later stage.

The development worker took a very active role in a number of inter-agency groups concerned with childcare issues following the implementation of the Children Act, including family support services, childcare provision, play schemes and leisure activities. There was a substantial flow of information across, within and between these groups. The Henley worker's aim was to act as far as possible as a catalyst for change, to enhance the effectiveness of liaison and commitment to consultation and partnership with parents and other local people. She continued to be involved with local people in gathering information about childcare needs in the area. The review — funded by the Social Services Department initially — has been described already. The B.A.C.C.S. was funded by the newly established Area Management Team, set up to improve coordination of local authority services and liaison with health and other agencies whose aims were relevant to the quality of life in the area.

From June 1992 a subgroup of the Area Management Team, involving the worker and parents from the Henley Project and members of other voluntary local groups and agencies, health, education and welfare workers, began to meet regularly to provide information to all agencies concerned with childcare and family support, to consider gaps in provision and ways of improving services.

Parents' views of their needs and those of their children, as well as their experience of services provided, were being discussed in this group and in a wide variety of other settings.

After this intensive period of gathering information the project was concerned with wide dissemination of findings. Information continued to be collected from some groups who had so far not been heard, and to supplement the information from parents with the views of local workers.

Black parents and white parents of Black children were involved during this period in meetings arranged through OSABA as well as the Black Access to Child Care Services review.

During 1993 and 1994 presentations of the project's findings were given to numerous, groups, including:
- local residents
- health, education and welfare workers and managers from the local area and city wide
- religious and voluntary groups
- police, probation, community safety and crime prevention workers
- local councillors and MPs
- at conferences and seminars throughout the UK, in Italy and Norway.

The work will be described in more detail in the following chapters. Outcomes and continuing influences of the work begun by the Henley Safe Children Project, in collaboration with many other groups, will be discussed in the final chapter.

3 Parents' perspectives

Parents in contact with the project painted a varied picture of life in the Henley area. Many had experiences of close neighbourly support and community involvement and expressed strong attachments to their neighbourhood. Nevertheless major stresses and difficulties were common, even for those who had strong networks of support. This chapter will focus on parents' experience and views of trying to bring up their children in the area. It will draw on interviews, discussions and group meetings with local parents — mostly mothers — who worked with us during the project.

Some of the characteristics of the neighbourhood have already been described. The disadvantaged environment summarised below was the ever present context of family life and childrearing.

Characteristics of the Henley Ward

- high unemployment; more than 40% of adults economically inactive
- in the most disadvantaged areas of the ward, over 40% of the population is aged under 18
- high proportion of low birthweight babies
- highest rate for city of accidents to children under 5
- very high number of children on child protection register
- highest rate of emergency hospital admissions:
  - particularly high for gynaecological and paediatric admissions
- average age of death earliest for the city
- crime highest in city including:
  - burglaries
  - criminal damage
  - sexual assault
- highest number of children in the care of the local authority

A recurring theme was the interconnection of personal difficulties and the social environment, reflecting closely the issues set out in chapter one.

In the Henley area many parents were afraid to let children out in public spaces on their own because of crime, drug dealing, bullying, dangerous debris and rubbish in open spaces and high rates of traffic accidents.

The two letters which follow were sent to the project by a mother who wanted her experience to be used, but did not want to attend a group meeting. They give a vivid impression of the conditions which some families found themselves in and how they felt about them.

I occupy a top floor, three bedroomed flat with my fiance and five children, who are aged from 14 years to 5 months.

In the last 2 months my fiance, who is on sick benefit, was mugged at knife-point and robbed, he and a friend who was visiting were beaten up while trying to stop our friend's van being stripped by a gang. This resulted in them being taken to hospital to be treated for concussion, cuts, bruises and stitches. Because we reported both incidents to the police, we are now being subjected to verbal abuse called from windows, and when my fiance was taken to Birmingham CID to look at photo-fit pictures, we came home to find we had been burgled. The police think that it could be connected to him being seen with a CID officer, who also heard the abuse shouted from a window.

I am being treated for post-natal depression and my health visitor has written to the council and my doctor is also writing because living in these conditions is aggravating the condition.

I have not been out of this flat for 2 months because I am too frightened.

When the children play out, they are picked on and bullied by older children, along with other small children who are likewise bullied. My son, who is thirteen and deaf, is bullied frequently and has his hearing aids pulled from his ears and is taunted because of his speech difficulties.

I have sent this letter so that I can tell you how it is for my family and it is very similar for others who live here.

You may think that it doesn't really matter but a lot of people that live here are decent people. How have they lived here for so long without going mad?

To live here is HELL on earth. How long have I been here you ask. Eleven of the longest MONTHS of my life.

•••••

I am sorry I was only able to write to you and not attend the meetings in person, but as I said in my letter, I do not feel safe and am frightened to go out, hopefully this will pass with time. My fiance and I are perfectly happy for you to pass our letter on to the names you sent us.

If you feel that my letter will be of some help, then by all means use it to make the 'decision makers' understand just what it is like for some families here, hopefully they will listen and not judge all of us by the same standard as the small minority of thugs that make people live like this.

We have now lived here for one year and hopefully the council will re-house us somewhere well away from here where my children can play safely outside without being taunted and bullied and where they won't have to paddle through the dirt and refuse that is frequently strewn over the paved area at the entrance. The council last year very kindly sent round a rota for the residents telling them when it was their turn to clean the communal bin area and landings in the flats. At that time, I was about 7 months pregnant and felt that as I took the trouble to buy black bin bags for my family's refuse, which I tied and deposited in the receptacles provided, I don't see why I should go out and wade through other people's dirt, waste food and filthy disposable nappies, just because they can't be bothered. Maybe I'm a snob, but pregnant or not, they have got a choice. I keep my home clean and don't object to brushing and mopping the landing, but I stop there.

I'm sorry this is another episode but this place needs sorting out, not just talked about and then shelved because after all, it's only Henley Green.

Thanks again for your letter.

Experience and views of parents

Over 275 parents — mainly white — were involved in giving information. Some of these were brought together in small groups. Some individual parents had detailed discussions with the development worker. Additional information was shared at steering group meetings. The views of 75 people were recorded in detail — 67 women, 8 men and 1 child. Parents were not asked for personal details, but of the 75 adults, 61 were known to be white, 5 were African Caribbean, 1 was Asian. Eight had children of mixed heritage. One parent was known to have a child with a hearing impairment.

We have also drawn on the 2 surveys of parents' childcare needs and resources, described in chapter 2, involving over 100 white parents, and 66 Black parents. A social work student placed with the development worker gathered additional information from parents city wide who had children with disabilities or were themselves disabled. She saw 35 parents for group or individual interviews: 32 mothers and 3 fathers. Four were themselves disabled: 2 male and 2 female. Nineteen of the mothers were of White European origins, thirteen of Asian origin. There were two Asian and one white man involved.

The processes involved in contacting and working with local people to document their views and become involved with workers and local groups interested in child care will be discussed in Chapter 5.

A group of six mothers remained in close contact with the project for more than 12 months, attending Steering Group meetings and taking part in the dissemination.

From the group discussions it was clear that there were enormous variations in circumstances and in range and level of contacts with health and welfare agencies. Some of the parents had had almost no contact with anyone apart from their GP. Some had had involvement with agencies in the past but were not currently using them, some had current involvement with statutory and voluntary agencies and some had very intensive involvement with several agencies.

Throughout the project there was a strong commitment to work flexibly, to facilitate, not restrict, what people wanted to say. Attempts were made to document exactly what was said rather than to interpret comments made. Flexibility about what was to be discussed was important because

- the project had been set up to demonstrate the value placed on parents as experts
- the project was committed to providing opportunities for parents themselves to decide what they wanted to say, and what should happen to the views expressed
- throughout the project many parents clearly stated that noone listened to them; others said if they were listened to, they were still not taken notice of.

Findings have been grouped under the following common themes:
- The social atmosphere
- The physical environment
- Resources and supportive services for families and children
- Resourcefulness in the face of stress overload
- Information needs
- Parents' priorities

The social atmosphere

Many parents stated that one of the good things about living in the Henley Green/Wood End/Bell Green area is the existence of a helpful, friendly community spirit:

> People are very helpful and help one another and they stick together the neighbours are friendly.

> Close community — good friends have stayed close friends.

However, many parents accompanied such statements with other comments, which suggest that running alongside this friendliness there is another, more negative and destructive atmosphere, leading to anxiety about what is expected of people and about who can be trusted.

Parents from the Henley Green area, when asked about difficulties in bringing up children in the area made the following comments:

> We used to be able to play in the street when about six, not now — don't know who is going to pick children up.

> We are worried about other children our children are going to mix with:
> - bad language
> - encouraged into vandalism, thieving, fighting.

There are lots of young children (4 years and above) on the street at inappropriate times of day and evening.

We see young (8 and over) children in charge of younger children — substitute mums.

Sometimes I think I'm abnormal for not letting my daughters play out in the area; being involved with the project has made me feel better about this; it has made me understand that I have good reason to watch them carefully.

When children are asked to other children's homes — wherever you live, not just Henley Green — you worry about:
• are they being watched by other child's parents
• you need to know parents are home
• are the other children allowed to go just anywhere.

We worry more (as adults) about making friends: we don't know what people are into, for example drugs.

Some parents want to keep themselves to themselves.

Do young women think of having children as a way out?

Fear and intimidation was a common experience:

Older children attacking younger children.

When you get broken into and things stolen you might know who has taken it but cannot report it further.

I'm worried about my own daughter, who has nothing to do and also my 12 year old son who was recently attacked at the local shops. His father went out but the youths then started to throw stones at him. I did not want to tackle the parents of these other children because I did not want further trouble for my own children.

On bonfire night, a group of families arranged a small bonfire and display by their homes. As the fire started to go out, a group of youths passing by decided to liven things up by tearing the fences to other people's homes down to re-kindle the fire — the families called the Police as the youths built the fire bigger and bigger. When the Police arrived, they said 'the youths were just having a bit of fun' — my 65 year old neighbour, who telephoned them as a law abiding citizen, was shocked at their reaction. They refused to move them on and extinguish the fire. She pointed out one person and was told that she shouldn't do things like that in public. Her reaction to me was 'why should I bother'? This resident was later subject to *intimidation* over several months.

It was clear from listening to parents talking about their experiences that some parts of the neighbourhood were more difficult to live in than others.

In the summer of 1991 the Community Safety Mediation Project held a workshop for residents in a small area of Wood End. The workshop, at which the Henley Safe Children Project worker was a facilitator, was set up to look at what it was like for people to live there and to see if any changes could be made. The women who came to the meeting all had children. They gave the following summary of their experiences of living in the area:

Feelings
- anger
- frustration
- isolation/imprisonment
- disgust
- fear for themselves and for their children's safety

Problems
- cars and motorbikes being driven dangerously
- burglaries — leading to fear of leaving anything valuable in an empty house and fear of leaving the house empty
- dumping stolen motorbikes and cars
- intimidation – both from young people and adults
    - verbal abuse and threats
    - by gathering in the street and attitude
    - by causing damage
- storing of and receiving of stolen property by residents
- isolation of young people
- young people being a law unto themselves — leading to properties and gardens not being safe
- recrimination/retaliation for being seen talking to police or if reporting a crime to the police — leading to fear of this
- neighbours who don't do anything
- message given to newcomers by the young people by intimidation, threats, physical violence, damage to property
- failing of system.

Suggestions for change
- development of a different sort of neighbourhood watch scheme tailored to the needs of the street;
- people to support each other;
- improved security of properties;
- development of communication system between neighbours

- underground telephone wires (some phone lines had been cut prior to offences)
- better communication between police and residents (not just when crime is reported), more contact with beat policemen
- more information about Crown Prosecution Service — how legal system works – feedback of what action is taken against offenders

Minority groups

Drop In Sessions were held by the project worker at a Family Centre during this period. Issues about racism were raised. One group of parents watched a video called 'Being White' then discussed their feelings and the issues it raised when focusing in on 'White' cultures instead of Black cultures. This group of parents also discussed issues about being assertive and being able to say no to partners, their children, their friends, their neighbours and local agency workers, when they thought this was needed.

They put forward a number of ideas to other Safer Cities projects and through the Community Safety Officer, for initiatives requiring a neighbourhood strategy, using a community development approach, rather than individualised responses.

As well as particular areas of the district being more difficult to live in than others, certain groups within the community faced extra dangers and harassment, particularly children from minority ethnic communities and children with disabilities. Parents reported:

It's not safe for children in their own back yard, neighbours have shouted racist abuse at children through the fence as well as poking sticks through the fence into her face.

One African Caribbean woman described how her mother who had lived in the same house for 25 years, had recently been suffering racial harassment. A fire was lit outside her front door and she had felt intimidated by groups of twelve to fourteen year olds (in gangs of six or more) and by neighbours leaving the pub. Sometimes she had heard fighting in the house next door and been too afraid to sleep.

This leaves my mum a nervous wreck – my daughter stays overnight with her sometimes. My Mum has dropped out of the neighbourhood watch.

African Caribbean women said they had to find support for their stressful circumstances in citywide organisations such as OSABA Women's Centre. They and parents of mixed race children had additional fears for the safety of their children on the street and even in their own homes, because of racism and prejudice.

One mother said she had to change her child's bedroom, because of other children playing on the roof of the shed.

After I called the police out I was broken into 3 times after this so I stopped calling the police.

This problem, and another one where neighbours were making drilling noises day and night, preventing a child sleeping, was associated with racist attitudes from neighbours.

It is worth noting here that several white parents mentioned moving their children's beds or strategically placing a wardrobe to prevent anything coming through a window and hurting their child. These were not parents who were being particularly harassed but parents who did this as a matter of course. For Black residents, such incidents are always experienced in relation to racism as a central part of their daily life.

A number of residents thought the police had unhelpful attitudes to Black people. Parents of mixed heritage children expressed concern about the implications of this for their children.

Some parents of mixed heritage children were also worried about the police practice of patrolling the area in groups — rather than twos — on foot. They said they felt as though they were being watched.

As a result of complaints to the housing department of racial harassment by their neighbours, one family was advised that they could be moved. The family's response to this was 'why should victims of racism move when nothing is done about the perpetrator?'.

An elderly Asian woman told the worker: 'my windows have been put in 3 times as a result of racial harassment'.

Another mother spoke of harassment of her family: 'people get picked on, hassled because of having a handicapped child'.

Street troubles

In the summer of 1992 there was a series of disturbances in the Wood End area of the Henley Ward, following an attempt by the police to challenge some of the antisocial behaviour of a small minority of young people, particularly around the use of motorbikes on footpaths and green spaces.

These disturbances raised many issues for local people and workers in the area, which tie in directly with some of the parents' views from the Henley Safe Children Project and the Mediation Workshop, about the social atmosphere in which they and their children have to live. One of the key issues that the disturbances raised was the way in which people from outside view Wood End residents. Many local residents felt outraged that all residents in Wood End were being labelled by the media as troublemakers or rioters. Some groups complained that the term 'riot' was used by the media instead of disturbance. They also felt that the media focused on the young people who caused the disturbances and their experiences rather than on finding out how other residents felt about the situation.

There was also anger and frustration that the 'other side' of the story was not easily available to the media. There were a number of people who felt pleased that the police were trying to deal with the behaviour and actions of a small number of motorbike riders (although they may not have agreed with the method used). Some of those who felt this way would have found it difficult to voice their views for fear of retaliatory action being taken against them or their children. As a result, many local residents' views about the disturbances and their causes were not heard and the complexity of the situation was not acknowledged.

Mothers whose children had narrowly missed being injured by motorcyclists whilst walking along the pavement, parents who dare not allow their children to play on grassed areas in front of their houses and flats because of risk of being knocked down by motorcyclists are just some of the local residents who believed their views were not represented in the media debate about the Wood End disturbances.

Stigma, labelling

Most parents had a perception that there was a stigma attached to living in Wood End, which was seen as the part of the Henley ward with the worst reputation. One mother stated that:

> Normally if you live in Wood End you are labelled as thick, that you don't care how you live, that you have no expectations or fears, are apathetic, don't work, have no manners, are not trustworthy and are deprived.

She went on to say that:

> Some of these labels are true for some people some of the time but everyone else has to live with these labels all of the time.

She gave as an example:

> I was working in a shop in town and my employers were shocked— that I lived in Wood End and my children were born there as they saw me as a well educated and competent person and my children were well mannered — my only thoughts were, well what do they expect me to be like.

Another mother stated:

> There are lots of people on the estate in the same situation as my family. Just because the area has a bad reputation for violence and criminal behaviour doesn't mean we are all the same.

Her view was:

> Other people look at you and think you deserve to be in this situation, that it's your fault and that you are happy living as you are and that you don't want to improve your life and the lives of your children. We feel we are

caught in a trap that we can't get out of, though you do learn to survive. But we don't want just to survive, we have standards too, we want a nice home, to be able to live amongst friendly respectable neighbours, have a clean tidy estate instead of looking out on piles of rubbish and litter.

Parents also frequently complained of 'job and credit applications being turned down if you put that you lived in Wood End'.

As well as feeling 'second class citizens', parents stated that it was hard work living in Wood End and even though there were positive things, 'things are getting worse and it is frightening'.

Some parents pointed out that 'there are no road signs to Wood End; Bell Green and Henley Green are sign posted'. They saw this as symptomatic of negative views of Wood End.

One mother claimed that although, as residents of Wood End, they were often labelled 'deprived' they had also been labelled as 'not deprived enough' by one voluntary organisation:

On one occasion we were invited by the W.I. from another area to a garden party for our children which they went on and thoroughly enjoyed, but, several days later we received a letter saying that the W.I. felt that the children were not deprived enough because they had shoes on their feet, and named track-suits, they were also well mannered. They felt that the following year that their efforts would be better spent on more needy families.

Parents' comments show how those who are trying to bring up their children in health and safety, as responsible members of the community, are doing so against very difficult odds. The conditions described — the alienation, destructiveness, negative and antisocial attitudes which sur-round families — create an atmosphere where parents and children live in stress and fear.

One parent summed this up:

We want our children to be happy and not feel threatened. Most of all we want our children to grow up into nice young people with morals and standards. We all want children in Wood End and Henley Green to have the right to grow up in a child friendly caring community and not feel second rate citizens because of the area they live in.

Even where the problems may come from a small minority, they may have an effect on the majority out of all proportion to the numbers involved. It is an effect which may be very difficult to counteract.

The Physical Environment

Positive Features

Parents identified a number of advantages to living in the area.

It's good that the shops are near at Bell Green, at Broad Street — though they are expensive.

We can walk to Sainsbury's and Asda.

There are good bus routes.

There is the Vanguard (private) bus service which is friendly, helps with buggies, shopping etc. and is cheaper by 1p.

There are fields and green space near us.

The countryside, animals and the canal are close by.

Problems

Parents described some of the difficulties linked to the physical environment which affected bringing up children in the area:

No phones working.

When I moved into a council house, the council had refused central heating to the last tenant. Therefore I had no central heating. No alternative heating was offered to me. I had a baby at the time.

When I moved into my house the fencing was not up. I have been waiting three years for the fencing to be put up.

I have no gate, therefore the children cannot play out.

Numerous residents mentioned that the design of the flats was a problem.

There are stairs in the flats where I live which make it difficult when I go out and I have my pram and shopping.

Then work is done in the area it isn't finished off properly — as if they don't care because it's Wood End or Bell Green.

Council workmen do not clear up after work — for example boards from windows, doors, broken glass.

There are ants in the flats — you need to pay £18 to Environmental Services to get rid of them.

The bin area should be enclosed with a gate.

In some lobbies/passages of our flats there is human and dog mess and nobody cleans it up. Residents do do it but it doesn't last, it has to be done straight away. Little children are ill as a result of this mess.

Children set light to newspapers which have been filled with dog mess outside people's front doors. They then knock on the door and run away. The tenant comes out and stamps on the newspaper to put out the fire and gets covered in dog mess.

There are 13-14 year olds peeing and glue sniffing in the lobby.

You have to take days off work to be in when they (Housing Dept) come round to do the repairs; then sometimes they don't come.

Motorbikes — when they are pinched they are taken to bits. These bits are left lying around. Children of 6-7 end up playing with these bits and end up covered in oil and with cuts.

There needs to be somewhere else for motorbikes to go.

Sweets and crisp wrappers etc., are left lying around outside the shop, and these go into the gardens.

There are no covers on the drains and children end up playing in them.

The doctors and dentists look shabby, dirty, unwelcoming.

The local dentist has gone private.

In Monkswood Close, the cars go round too fast, this means that children cannot play outside on their own, it's too dangerous.

Living in a 2nd floor maisonette I can't let my child out to play because the grassed area isn't enclosed and it's near a main road.

The maisonette's balcony — he can climb over it and stick his head through it.

I wanted a house, was offered a house in one street, but didn't want to take that because it was depressing, muddy and dirty, the property was musty and badly decorated; I would have had to do a lot of work and spend money on it — it's far from town — 3 miles or so.

There are not enough bins in flats or on lamp posts.

Rubbish gets dumped on the green and set on fire.

There's nowhere safe for children to play.

Stray dogs were a source of anxiety to some residents.

Few suitable buildings, available for children's activities, were identified.

A household survey done in August 1992 as part of the Henley Green Street Project (by the City Council's Economic Development Department) found:

- • 91 residents strongly supported an area clean up with skips, an opportunity to dispose of bulky household rubbish.
- • 78 residents strongly supported improvements to children's play facilities.

Ninety-nine forms were returned for this survey, which represented a response rate of only 13.9%.

In all the groups organised in the Henley Project there was a strong priority expressed for having parks in the area, where people could mix more easily with other members of the community, and where there would be more supervised activities and play space for children. Parents described their hopes for safety in the community: they were interested in finding ways to improve safety on the streets, from cars, people, other children — even sometimes from themselves, acknowledging the very real risks which parents who are tired and stressed can pose to their children.

Resources and support services for families with children

Parents were asked to identify any positive family support services for those living in Wood End, Henley Green and Bell Green. They identified:

In Wood End

Princess Ann visiting us, the children got to meet her. (In February 1992, Princess Ann opened a new Family Project in the area funded under the Urban Programme, the Save the Children Fund and the Church Urban Fund. The new Wood End Family Project, with its purpose built centre, was seen as an important focus for community activity, providing a range of supports).

The Outreach Flat, where people gave you support. (A Community Education Project).

Getting information, meeting people and groups at the nursery.

Lots of groups going on, but they may not be easy to get in to.

There are lots of schools plus nurseries within walking distance.

In Henley Green

The school facilities, the parents' evening, you get to hear about computers being introduced.

The schools are near.

Facilities which parents already knew about in Henley Green included:

> The mother and tots group at Annie Osborne School, one afternoon a week. Parents organise it and use the school nursery equipment. You can play with your children there. The group gets support from Eburne Community Education Centre.

Four other mother and toddler groups were known about, each once a week. Local Authority nursery provision was appreciated. The loss of a playbus was regretted.

> Behaviour management classes run at Annie Osborne, there is a creche. I have been several times, it's good to have reminders. You get company and a break from your children. It gives you time for yourself. You can learn something plus there is a creche.

> There was a maths and English class at Eburne, not enough turned up at Annie Osborne to have a class there. I would have preferred a class at Annie's as it is too far to go to Eburne. I didn't attend the class as a result.

> The Business Skills course at the Outreach Centre. After Christmas couldn't make it because the hours were too long. I needed to collect my children from school.

A range of other events and facilities which they had heard of from workers in the area were mentioned, including community bonfires, tenants' consultations.

Health and welfare services

Parents described mixed experiences with health and welfare services. Some had had substantial support from health, education and social workers and other welfare professionals. Others took the view:

> There was nothing for me when I needed it.

The following comments from parents — again mainly mothers — represented the range of views:

> All agencies need to examine the way they are viewed by the public.

> I went to Social Services and I didn't get help.

> Social Services need to acknowledge people's views of them.

> Housing — I got help quickly.

> Housing, if you are nice you don't get anywhere, if you shout or swear, you get results sometimes.

My son has had lots of trouble being bullied at school and I have had problems getting him to go back to school.

Sex education in schools doesn't talk about emotions, it's very practical but doesn't talk about responsibilities after birth.

Doctors and health visitors give you conflicting opinions.

People have to wait a long time for a Doctor to come out to them when they have called one in.

I have letters saying that my Doctor will strike me off his list because I have called an emergency Doctor out.

The children have had illness, sickness, diarrhoea, linked to where they live and play, as well as animals. The doctor has advised me to change doctors because they have had to give too much time and medicine to my family.

There are problems in parents not having transport to get to appointments and when they do arrive with their children, there is nothing for the children to do while they are waiting.

Too much money has been shoved into the area and then left — residents are supposed to feel grateful for this.

In discussion with a small group of local mothers about the high numbers of children from the area who were seen at the casualty department and the high number of emergency admissions, a view that some doctors' attitudes to Wood End people were very negative was expressed. One mother stated her firm belief that the high rate of emergencies and unplanned hospital admissions noted in the area (see Chapter 2) were in part encouraged by some doctors' attitudes. Doctors were not taking children's and women's complaints seriously and were not referring cases on for further examination. Hence parents' own views about their and their children's health were being devalued, or ignored, resulting in greater use of the emergency services. Calling out the emergency deputising service was often necessary, she thought, because a general practitioner had been unsympathetic.

Minority groups said better information was needed about their health needs. The example of the need to test for sickle cell anaemia before having an anaesthetic was one of the examples used — medical and lay people were thought to be ignorant of this and other conditions which were common in their communities.

Issues that parents, usually women, from the Drop In sessions wanted to explore particularly during this period were understanding their and their children's health needs better. They arranged a visit to the Women's Health Information Centre as well as inviting speakers to talk to them about their and their children's health. They were also interested in looking at how to make food appealing to children, as well as learning how to cook new meals.

Priorities for support in the area

Parents involved in the group discussions identified these priorities:

* Parks and safe play areas.
* Child friendly facilities are needed everywhere so that it's comfortable to have your children with you at:
  doctors
  hospitals/clinics
  shopping eg.
  - help with doors
  - stairs
  - leaving pushchairs
  - check outs
  - wider shop aisles
  - making up an order if you go with a list.
* Children need to have positive experiences of visits to the doctors and hospitals.
* A babysitting service, cheap reliable babysitter, day or night.
* Counselling for children.
* Counselling for parents.
* Childcare support for parents when
  - working
  - shopping
  - needing respite
  - for emergencies
  - training.
* Cheap transport; a community bus or taxi with a driver so that you can go shopping — to buy in bulk, therefore get things cheaper, and for hospital visits.
* Pick up/drop off points for children who go to activities — so that the whole family doesn't have to go.

Parents at Drop In sessions described how difficult it was to go out for the day if you have children under 5 and no car. They felt strongly that lack of money, lack of transport, difficulties of using public transport with young children and buggies made it impossible to attempt trips out. However, they believed that families could really benefit from trips out together when children are young, as this is often a stressful time for them.

More places to go for older children, 7-11, 11-18, nearer to where they live.

> Boys' groups as well as girls' groups.

> There needs to be more and more people involved — spreading the word — less apathy — breaking down barriers between professionals and local volunteers.

> Should look at the needs of older children and unmarried mums, should be different opportunities for young women.

> Parents have a lot to offer but sometimes this is not asked for. They would like to do a lot more. It felt sometimes as if parents were asked to have a little dabble but cannot actually jump in.

One parent talked specifically about her experiences when she was having difficulties with the behaviour of one of her children. She outlined the support she felt she needed.

> There should be support for the child — independent; emotional support for parents. Someone to talk to — independent — and for you — a shoulder to cry on.

> Workers involved should have an understanding of how parents usually deal with their children (including an awareness of parents' income levels) and give back up and help to enforce parents' judgements and authority.

She had felt that her authority had been undermined when a worker had been insensitive to her income level. The worker had taken her child to MacDonalds for a meal which she could never afford to do. She emphasised that:
This support should be available for as long as the parent and child need it. Eventually she received helpful support from a social worker, from a child psychologist and the school, and a lot of advice from a behaviour management course. She explained:

> It is very important that they listen to parents as well as they listen to children ... as my child didn't seem to be making any progress, even though some work was being done, I called for an assessment to be done.

This led to more extensive work. From the time the assessment started she felt supported by the school. Her experience of trying to get help had however been extremely stressful. She did not feel that she got any practical help, which would have been of great benefit.

Resourcefulness in the face of stress overload

Whilst talking to parents, particularly parents who were struggling with longterm stresses or going through a difficult patch, it became clear how wide a range of problems they sometimes had to overcome. Having to deal with a multitude of difficulties at the same time was particularly stressful. Stress itself could cause more problems or bring people to the end of their tether, when their coping strategies would begin to crumble.

This was particularly evident for some of the individual parents who approached the development worker to write up their experiences. The mother who wrote the letters at the beginning of this section outlined some of her pressing family difficulties. Experiences of other families are described below.

Family One

This is a married couple with three children 4, 2 and 1, (one of twins where one was lost after 4 months pregnancy). The mother was 6 months pregnant and at the time the family described it had been a good pregnancy so far. The family are living on benefits. The mother's family had once had her and the children for a holiday, but wouldn't be willing to have her again with the children. They have no links with father's family.

Their account begins between 10.00 and 11.00 am one morning.

What happened — father's view

Day one — wife's waters broke
- husband found a babysitter (unpaid) to sit with wife and children
- went to get doctor (no phone in house)
- doctor came straight out and said wife needed to go into hospital immediately; he called for an ambulance which arrived within 15 minutes.

The father was then left with the decision whether to
- go with wife and leave children with babysitter/friend that he was not particularly happy about leaving his children with on their own, or:
- stay with children and not go with wife.

He had to make this decision and deal with things calmly so that his wife didn't panic.

He chose to go to hospital — and waited until his wife was settled in.

He then rang a local church group which he attends, explained the situation to them and asked for someone to go and take over from the babysitter until he could get home.

The church group coped for the rest of the day and also picked him up in the evening from the hospital. As he did not have a phone he left the phone numbers of the church group and two friends with the hospital.

He didn't know how long his wife was going to be in hospital for — it could be for anything up to three months.

He had normally helped his wife with the care of the children but she had done more with them than he had.

Day Two — The father tried to set up a routine involving the care of the children, and described his concerns:
• worried that other people might think he wasn't coping with the children
• didn't want to neglect the children
• he wanted to make hospital visits
• wanted to keep the house clean and tidy for the children, also for visitors
• wanted to have time to spend with the children — who were upset about mum not being there
• new routine didn't work because the children's original routine was gone and they didn't really understand why. They would wake up in the night — perhaps 1 a.m. — upset and wouldn't go back to sleep
• the husband had had offers of help from neighbours and friends when his wife had gone into hospital but none ended up giving any
• the church group helped out but this meant fitting into their timescales

The following days — The children went off their food, he was worried that they weren't eating, so went to the doctors with the children. A health visitor came round to talk to him about the children. She gave advice and suggested what to do. He still had to do household tasks, e.g. pay bills, do the shopping, washing, at the same time as looking after three children. He was still having disrupted sleep every night.

The church group organised a birthday party for one of the children so that she didn't miss out because her mum was in hospital. Mum was in hospital for a month and he had to keep up the routine come what may — so that he could keep on top of everything. He hated the evenings — the children would be in bed and he would be on his own with time to think and worry.

He had kept one child going to her nursery and got extra time for her there, but he still had to go backwards and forwards to drop her off and collect her, taking the other two children with him. When visiting his wife with the children he had limited time to see her and talk properly, as he had to supervise three small children who found it difficult to sit still for very long. He couldn't let them run round the ward.

When his wife came out of hospital she needed looking after — as she had had a Caesarian and sterilisation and needed to take it slowly. Everybody then came to visit the baby. Just before she came out of hospital, he had been to Social Services and explained the situation because he was worried that she could be suffering from post natal depression (she had done so in the past). Social Services said that she would get help if she needed it. He went back to Social Services when he started to see signs of post natal depression but did not get any help.

The health centre were keeping an eye on the new baby and mother — there were worries about the baby's low weight and mother had difficulties breast feeding because of stress and depression. The baby was referred to the doctor who then sent her straight to the hospital: going in on Friday and coming out on Monday. He went to visit in the evenings and his wife went to visit in the mornings — this involved feeding and looking after the baby while there. The church group gave lifts to the hospital. When the baby was home she was fed every three hours. He was desperate for sleep throughout this period.

Father's feelings — He said that he felt distraught, with great uncertainty about how long the situation was going to go on. He was worried about his wife and baby surviving. He felt exhausted; his feelings were building up, he was not eating properly. He experienced great frustration about asking for help and not getting it. He was lonely and worried, with no-one to talk to. What kept him going was love of his wife and children and his efforts to keep to a routine. If the situation had gone on any longer he didn't know what would have happened.

Help and support he would have liked — He felt he needed support during the day; once in a while someone to take care of the children for 2 hours while he did some jobs, such as shopping. He would have liked someone to talk to once the children were in bed. He particularly wanted answers to questions when he asked them. The hospital and health centre had different weights for baby and he didn't know which one was right. If this had been sorted out it might have stopped baby going into hospital.

He needed a response from Social Services: they said they would send somebody, but they didn't say who or when and no-one came. He would have liked more time on his own when visiting his wife at the hospital, so would have welcomed some way of having the children cared for at the hospital for some visits.

Mother's concerns and feelings

If her husband hadn't gone with her, he would have had to find someone else to go with her to the hospital, so that there was someone who would let him know what was going on.

When she was put on a drip to stop her labour, noone explained for two days why they had done this. She was terrified and angry because she wanted to go home to see her other children, yet wanted to finish her labour.

When she asked why her waters had broke — they didn't say. She had to ask why labour was being stopped. Staff did eventually explain that they were trying to take the baby from 32 to 34 weeks so that the lungs would have developed properly.

They waited two more days to make the decision about whether to do a Caesarian or normal delivery as the baby was in the breach position.

She didn't see her own consultant until she had been there for a week — she saw the consultant's 'understudy'.

While waiting she didn't feel ill but was bored and kept wondering what was going on.

A Caesarian section which was set for the 24th October was brought forward to the 22nd because of an infection. She was told at lunchtime on the 22nd that she would have her operation at 6.00 pm. Her husband had visited her with the children so he had to take them back to Wood End and then come back. While she was waiting she felt really nervous. The operation was fully explained to her. She had the baby at 6.25 pm. The baby was jaundiced and was in special care for two days.

There was confusion about the birth weight of the baby at the hospital.

When she came back from hospital on Sunday there was a nonstop stream of visitors who came to see the baby, not her, and stayed sometimes for long periods. Very soon after she had left hospital someone asked her to babysit for their children, making her feel that there had been very little recognition of how precarious their whole situation had been.

Two months later the development worker spoke to the mother and father together. They continued talking of their experiences:

Having this baby was different because it was premature — 2 months early, therefore planning for the baby's arrival was thrown out, for example money, and clothes.

The birth happened 12 weeks before the baby grant was due and they hadn't had the £100 maternity grant. The father had to go and sort this out whilst he had his three children with him. He had to travel to the Social Security Office. They had no clothes in for a premature baby — these clothes are more expensive. The mother talked to the friend of a friend who had had a premature baby and swapped clothes — they begged and borrowed clothes.

The mother had had a Caesarian section and was also sterilised at the same time and she felt that she was just getting over it, after two months, that her body was just getting back to normal. She had to go back on iron tablets — she was still feeling *tired and exhausted*. The baby wouldn't wake up on her own for her three hour feeds; she got an eye infection which needed syringing; she needed to have soya milk. The mother was stressed and had post natal depression; the stress of all this affected the relationship between the mother and father. They said that for a time there was no communication, no talking.

They felt that people were expecting too much of them: for example neighbours borrowing nappies.

'We just must manage — don't make a fuss — everybody thinks that you can cope because you don't complain. The children get second hand clothes from the church as we can't afford new ones for them all. We asked for a crisis loan — refused it. We had no cakes, trifles etc., for Christmas.'

The oldest child, who attends nursery, kept asking mother why they didn't have special Christmas food.

'We are now putting away money for 2 hampers through the Provident for next year.'

The children's sleep was irregular, their routines upset. 'There is no time on your own.' They felt the youngest child had had to grow up very quickly.

Their second youngest child had had an allergic reaction to milk, but this had taken six months to be discovered.

'We worry about illness as the baby was premature. We were given a cook book about how to cook with soya, but no diet sheets. We've claimed for a special diet allowance from the Social. We are living in a two bedroomed flat so we have overcrowding. We have arrears so can't move. We are paying off arrears but slowly. Youngest gets out of cot and joins others in their beds.'

There was a problem about their tenancy, because of an error on the computer. It appeared that they had two separate tenancies, therefore the second tenancy was still in arrears. Their housing officer was trying to sort it out but there was a delay at the Department head office. The amount owed was approximately £300, but the housing office were not sure of the precise amount.

Other points that the parents made were:

'The family project worker was more help than friends.'

'I don't ask for help from Social Services unless I need it — I know when I need help.'

The father's mother and father were known to Social Services when he was a child, which worried him, making him wonder whether Social Services would be watching him more closely because they had been involved with other family members.

The difficulties this family experienced in getting support from neighbours needs to be understood in the light of general pressures in the neighbourhood, and high proportion of children and young people in the area compared to adults; more than 40% under 18 compared to a national average of 25%.

Garbarino (1980) described increased risks of harm to children in neighbourhoods where it was difficult to access informal networks of support. Gibbons (1990) has described how helpful parents found it to have ready access to a range of supportive services in a neighbourhood.

The Social Services Team had very high referral rates for child abuse investigations (See Chapter 2) and had little time to offer support in such situations. They worked closely with the Henley project, however, to review neighbourhood needs and work to develop strategies of family support for the area. A recurring theme in our discussions with parents was the importance of *defining their own needs*; being taken seriously *when they said they needed help and support* rather than being dependent on a professional worker's assessment, or the rationing priorities of agencies.

Family Two

A mother with two children, aged 2 and 5 when she came to Wood End, now almost grown up, described her views and experience. She had been an active campaigner in getting some of the most dilapidated housing knocked down. Some of the good things she had experienced about living in Wood End had been:

'Children were better behaved then — neighbours were very helpful — if you needed help they were there — it wasn't far to go to the shops — we used CB radio to talk to each other.'

'If you had one break-in, that was it. I had help from Victim Support — which was a turkey, children's presents and a basket of fruit.'

She had experienced a wide range of difficulties in bringing up her children:

'There was nothing for the kids, no playing fields, facilities for all ages.'

'I had problems with my children. I had behaviour problems with the older child, they told school that they had been smacked and the school told the welfare. We had family sessions at Far Gosford Street Centre which helped. I learnt to use no TV and no tuck at school with my child.'

This mother left Wood End when one of her children was sexually abused by her father. She went to the police when she found out about it. Her daughter had been buggered and raped. The father went to prison but still kept writing letters asking her to go back to him. When the tenants' association found out about her daughter's sexual abuse, they asked her to leave.

She then met a Northern Irish man who became redundant and wanted to go back to Northern Ireland. She and her daughter went with him. Whilst in Northern Ireland her daughter, now 9, made another complaint of sexual abuse which was dealt with by the NSPCC. Her daughter then went into care.

After this happened in Northern Ireland, she returned to Wood End, only to be driven out of Wood End a second time, when she and her new husband were allocated a house in Wood End which had other people's stuff in it, who had done a moonlight flit. Her new husband was given the keys by the housing officer and went to visit the flat. Whilst at the flat her husband was beaten up by the previous flat tenant. They had very serious threats made against them, and were eventually transferred to another area of Coventry.

The case study of family 1 particularly shows how having to deal with unanticipated difficulties can result in parents' day to day coping strategies breaking down. It also demonstrates that parents would be able to cope much better if specific kinds of help and support could be made available when they need it. They were fortunate that there was some support for them from a local church organisation and a local worker when they needed it, but they also felt that they badly needed other forms of help and support which they weren't able to get. Both studies show how desperate the situation can be at times for families with few resources and limited networks of support. Parents' ability to provide safe, stable caring environments for their children can be stretched beyond endurance at times of crisis.

Issues for parents

Several themes came through from these case studies. Even when parents have high expectations for their children, they can be thwarted by circumstances which are outside their control. Sometimes parents who have been involved in supporting the local community, for example through reporting criminal activity, being actively involved in improving housing conditions, supporting other families with their childcare, cannot rely on having their community's support when they most need it. These families and others had suffered:

- retaliation for reporting criminal activity — burglary and intimidation;
- being asked to leave a tenants' association because of offences committed against them;
- friends not returning support to the parents when they most needed it; not always being reliable.

The two families described here and the one in the letter beginning this chapter had some help from agencies in the area, but did not feel that this was enough, in relation to what was happening to them, and it was not necessarily available at the time they felt near to a crisis.

In two of the case studies, parents felt abandoned, left to deal with very difficult and stressful situations alone. Their anger and frustration clearly came through. The practical demands on them would tax the most well resourced families, yet they were having to manage with minimal resources and support.

This anger and frustration is also echoed in the following comments made by parents with children who were in care or supervised by Social Services:

I've tried my best and my best isn't good enough.

My family of four are expected to live in a bedsit designed for one person. There is no space for me to get away from things where I live. You are being tested to see if you can live under pressure, if you can get through this you must be OK.

Recommendations of the case conference mean that:
- parents: they have to do everything that is recommended or else there will be consequences, for example, if you don't take your children to hospital
- Social Services: they can promise services to parents that they then can't or don't provide, such as parents being told that they can have one night out a week, but this never happens. It is very difficult when you get conflicting advice from professionals, for example as a first time mum about feeding your baby.

Cries for help are ignored until something happens; parents should be able to call for a review.

Accumulation of stress

Family Three

The long term experience of a family with a child who is disabled gives a vivid impression of how stress may accumulate over years, and come from many directions. One mother interviewed had three children (all female), one of whom is disabled. The child had been diagnosed as having a condition called Sturge Weber, which affects the brain and results in memory loss. In addition, the young girl was identified as having epilepsy.

The girl's mother was critical of the treatment of her child by professionals, from the moment she was born to the present day.

The criticisms centred upon professionals' lack of understanding and inability to take on board parental worries and concerns. The mother found professionals dismissive and unsympathetic. Knowing that her child was not developing in the same way as her first daughter, she made her worries known to a paediatrician 'who fobbed me off by telling me that nothing was wrong with her'. There followed a long period of inaction during which time the child's health deteriorated until it was finally recognised that she had 'Sturge Weber'.

The mother's comments in summarising her experiences of the medical profession are revealing about the status of parents in decision making processes:

'The whole problem is that you are not listened to; the only person who knows a child is the parents, because they live with them 24 hours a day.'

In trying to communicate some of these fears, the mother said she was met with the stereotypical statement that she was simply 'being a neurotic mother'.

She spoke at length of the feeling of alienation from her own child, and associated fears and concerns in 'handing her child over' as it were, to the realm of the professional.

This was particularly the case in all the dealings she and her partner had with the psychologists. She recounted how it felt to watch her own daughter being 'taken away to have assessments made'. The whole process rendered them powerless in the care and treatment of their daughter, they felt.

They identified four main causes of their experience of powerlessness:

1) Professional detachment and inability to hear and take on board the early concerns of the parents about their daughter's development and health.

2) Their understanding and knowledge of their child, was felt to be devalued and undermined by a medicalised perspective, which was deemed to be more credible than a parent's instinctive responses and continual daily contact with their child.

3) The parents found the medical profession to be generally non participatory, leaving them feeling that they were not properly or significantly informed of their daughter's illness, and the future health implications for her.

4) The psychologist's attempt to put their daughter into 'convenient' categories, which denied her any individuality. It was felt that once a medical label had been assigned to their daughter, it was difficult to register any differences from the 'norm', ie. their daughter as an individual became lost to a powerful and alienating label. It was felt that the allocation of a medical label served only to make the lives of doctors/consultants easier, and that it had no real positive effects for their daughter.

The mother believed that there were certain practical steps that could be taken to empower parents who have children who are disabled. During discussion she made these points:

1) That doctors should inform parents immediately that their child is suspected to have, or is diagnosed as having, some form of disability. The mother found that there was much reluctance on the part of the medical profession about committing themselves to a diagnosis or sharing their thinking. She commented '... they don't want to tell you'. She believed that '... they should listen to your wishes rather than just what they think'. A more mutual sharing, exploratory, approach was being recommended.

2) The mother suggested that parents should '... be there when making assessments, either actually in the room, or behind a two way mirror, to share expertise and challenge feelings of powerlessness'.

3) She felt that professionals could offer more reassurance. The mother believed that it would have been helpful for their worries and concerns to have been taken seriously. Instead they often found themselves left in the dark, or labelled as overanxious, interfering parents.

4) She felt strongly that parents should be involved in every decision as it was they who knew their child best. '... The people who make decisions have got no idea about what the real world is like.' She felt that there was a need for professionals to be more aware of the daily reality of living with disability in a family.

5) The mother recommended that '... each child should be treated as an individual, and that professionals should avoid placing children into convenient categories which denies them their individuality'.

Societal reactions The mother also talked about the difficulties they had encountered as parents at a societal level. Other people's perceptions were often judgmental and critical. As there was no overt manifestation of the young girl's disability, her parents felt they had to contend with a multitude of prejudicial remarks. Often if the young girl's behaviour was difficult or unmanageable as a result of her medical condition, it was seen as being 'your fault as a parent for not being able to control your children.'

There were occasions when her daughter's disability remained undetected, making her feel that she had to justify the concessions that she got as a parent with a child who is disabled. For example, the family is in receipt of an orange badge for their car, notifying that a passenger is disabled. Often, because their daughter's disability was not immediately apparent, people questioned, .'...why has she got a pass?' This made the mother '...feel guilty,' although she knows she shouldn't. It is these daily occurrences and points of contact which denote a lack of societal awareness around disability and add to other difficulties experienced.

Accessibility of services and support The mother also noted that they (the parents) had continually had to fight for everything, be it allowances or which school their daughter was to attend. The young girl was originally placed at one school against the wishes of her parents, who believed that she would have difficulties in coping.

It was their wish that she would be transferred to a school which they felt to be more appropriate to her needs. They believed that change only came about because they fought for what they felt was best for their child. In doing so, they met with a lot of barriers, and were made to feel that they were doing it the wrong way, because they were not being compliant with the professional prognosis.

Safety issues Issues regarding her child's safety were of paramount importance for the girl's mother. She said '... she has no awareness of danger', that she '... can't leave her' for a moment since she would 'run away'. It is an issue that the mother believes will become even more difficult as her daughter gets older.

The mother had particular concerns for her daughter's health, safety and wellbeing with the onset of adolescence and sexual awareness and activity. She worried that her daughter might be vulnerable to abuse, and be '... unable to communicate it to her'.

The family found two sources of support, in what they saw as an otherwise unsympathetic and ignorant world: a respite care centre and the Sturge Weber Foundation.

Family Four

Another example of stress accumulating over time, as well as being present day by day, was given in an interview with a mother who is visually impaired and a father who is blind. They are the parents of two teenage children. During the interview, they recalled some of the difficulties they encountered as 'blind' parents.

Looking back on her and her husband's experiences, the mother sees it as having been 'damned hard work, bringing them up. We have to work very hard at bringing up our children,"... because we are disabled, people are more critical'.

She highlighted three major obstacles which they have had to face during the course of their children's development.

1) Safety

Safety was of paramount importance for both parents. Being visually impaired necessitated that they developed their own methods for keeping their children safe. It was imperative for them: '... to know where they were all the time', and they had to be '... insistent on holding their hands'.

Both parents found that 'being blind' presented difficulties in negotiating the layout of the house without falling on, or over, their children. As a result, it made them '... more conscious of safety with them', and aware of the need to develop their own '... ways and means around these problems'. 'A safety gate on the kitchen door to stop her coming in' for example, was one device used by the mother to prevent her daughter from entering the potentially dangerous environment of the kitchen.

They felt that they had to prove that as blind people, they were able to look after their children safely, often going against public opinion and professional judgement.

2) Getting help and support

According to the mother 'There is a great need for help and support for parents with children under 5'. Their experiences, however, of getting help and support were fairly mixed.

Both parents viewed their situation as perhaps slightly different from some other parents who are disabled. They said they were very articulate and so could ask for help, whereas for a lot of parents who are unaware of services and channels of information and communication, access to services can remain a mystery. Even they still had to '... work hard at getting help'.

There was also a perceived imbalance between inaction and interference from agencies. They felt there was no middle ground to engage services in a supportive capacity. The mother commented that services could be either '... over helpful or waited until you get into difficulties'.

Engaging services required persistence and determination in getting what they actually required. The mother gave as an example of this continual battle:

'We didn't want our daughter to go into care whilst I was in hospital, (having her second child). By being firm about it, we got what we wanted, more or less.'

Commenting on the actual quality of the service delivery, the mother had the following comments to make in relation to Health Visitors: 'The Health Visitor was good, but the service not particularly good. Health Visitors need to be more aware of the problems we have as disabled parents.'

She felt she had to find her own methods over problems of feeding, whereas she would have welcomed support.

As with all the difficulties they encountered as parents with sensory impairments, they found that '... a bit of thought and imagination can go a long way,' that there '... are ways and means around these problems'.

Often, parents who are disabled, or who have children who are disabled, rely heavily on the support of their own parents in helping to care for their children. This was not an option for either the mother or father interviewed, as their own parents lived long distances away. Most of their support came from 'Crossroads', a carers' support group.

Another difficulty mentioned by the mother was the role of her children as carers, a role she thought was imposed upon her daughter by Social Service's expectations that she would do the shopping from the age of 10 onwards: '... children shouldn't be responsible for the care of their parents, ... there should be more support for disabled parents with children'.

Being aware of the issues around children as carers, they were determined not to allow their children to perform the bulk of the domestic tasks, thus ensuring that: '... our own children haven't lost out'.

For other parents with disabilities, their children may be the only source of domestic support they have. They may not be able to avoid taking on the role of carer.

The mother felt that there was a need for professionals to give attention to the following:

- Consultants and Paediatricians don't understand the psychological problems facing parents who are disabled in bringing up their children.
- We need more help and support without being patronised and without sympathy.
- More home help support so children aren't expected to do the shopping and cleaning.

- More support from Social Services Departments, but in a way that is not interfering.
- Care Relief — respite care.
- Holidays, to give people a break.

3) Coping with people's attitudes

The mother believed that attitudes to disability were mostly negative and uninformed. Frequently she met with prejudicial comments, such as '... isn't it a shame'. Very often she and her partner got the distinct '... impression that (we) shouldn't have children.'

Sometimes this prejudice was directed at the children. Their son would get harassment from other children at school, who used his parents' disabilities as the target for their bullying. This caused tremendous strain and stress, not only to the boy, but also to his parents, who felt that the school was not addressing the bullying.

The mother felt that the only way to challenge people's stereotypes and inbuilt prejudices around disability, is to ensure: 'integration at an early age,' and in this way, 'we wouldn't get bullying and unkindness to each other.'

The parents recounted their good experiences: 'It's been hard work and challenging. We've proved it's possible to bring up a child.'

These detailed accounts have been used to illustrate the continuous relentless practicalities and emotional demands of bringing up children. Parents continuously demonstrated the interconnections of personal and social factors, stressing how important it was that individual workers should see their lives in the round, not in fragmented pieces (Blackburn, 1991 and 1992). Equally they hoped that agency policy and practice could reflect such an overview.

For families already experiencing severe stresses, any additional day to day problems associated with living on low incomes in an area where they and their children don't feel safe, can tip families into stress overload. One parent gave a common view:

Most of us love and care for our children and want the best for them. We can't always give them what they want or would like, and occasions like birthdays and Christmas are our worst nightmares.

Another said:

We want to be able to shop, to visit friends, to go on training courses, to work without worrying whether homes have been burgled when we get back.

One mother commented to the development worker, when she was asked about anything that could be done to support her getting to sessions, that she would

like someone to house sit for me so that I can leave the house without it being burgled.

This was even more important to her than childcare support.

Difficulties and achievements

Two other groups who worked with the development worker identified issues and difficulties they had in bringing up children in the area, and some of the things which had helped them to cope.
Difficulties included:

> Losing my temper and shouting.
> When I smacked my son.
> I wish I had not had my children so close together.
> I wish I hadn't made a favourite of my middle son — I think it made things harder for my eldest.
> Leaving one child out when the other was in hospital.
> Started having them later — having them young made things more complicated and harder for me.
> I would have liked to have been older

There were many times when parents felt they needed support in bringing up their children and they didn't get it. They mentioned:

> I did not get any support from anyone when my oldest daughter treats me like dirt and hurts my feelings.
> Post natal depression for 6 months.
> As a single parent going through a divorce I got no support.
> I would like some support right now while I feel that I hate my two older children.
> Had no support whatsoever — only 'family' in Coventry were my inlaws — who refused to babysit.
> I got no support from my mum.
> Family Doctor didn't listen to me when my child was ill.

Things which parents felt they had done well included:

> Coping with children through marriage and divorce.
> I felt proud having my children in the first place.
> Coping with twins without an extended family to help and advise.
> When my children had been in a school play or anything they have done in school.
> Feel proud of my sons — they've turned out OK in spite of bringing them up on my own from 16.
> Feel proud of my 4 kids (I started having them at 15). I proved everyone wrong — they thought I was mad.
> Still married with a nice family.
> Coped with situations mostly alone.
> Child's good school report.

Children using manners and not swearing.

They also outlined some of the sources of support which had been available when they needed it:

The Outreach project was just like an extended family — Bell Green Nursery — Crisis Intervention Team.

Outreach Centre helped me to grow.

Breaks from looking after them when they were in Outreach creche.

Wood End workers and residents.

Child behaviour management course.

Other mothers in play group.

I had support from my friends when I kicked my husband out.

Support from my partner, mum, friends — talking about what I'm doing — groups, classes — gave me confidence. Health Visitor helped with the oldest.

Support from the hospital and doctor and my husband when my youngest daughter had been ill.

Mum is also there to support and help in any situation.

Throughout the project many parents — particularly mothers — gave each other help and support when needed. When one of the group was ill and housebound another parent would often pick up children under 5 and bring them along to the creche, thus allowing the sick parent space at home alone.

Informal supports

Informal support was particularly important for one parent who became seriously ill during the project. One of her friends, also a group member, regularly took care of her child when she wasn't well enough to cope. Her illness was eventually diagnosed as Multiple Sclerosis. Once her illness was diagnosed this mother managed to negotiate support services, however the informal support received from one group member, readily accessible at the time of need, was invaluable.

Some group members lived next door or very close to each other. When there was trouble on the streets near them, it was helpful that they always knew that there was someone near watching out for them — especially when telephone lines were deliberately cut before trouble started.

Throughout the project there were frequent examples of local people supporting each other through difficult times — where informal networks of support were crucial to a family's ability to cope. The local family project was committed to provide help and support for such networks, and provided a local meeting place which was convenient and encouraging, facilitating a number of selfhelp projects.

Parents views about the lack of help when they were experiencing major problems or stress overload reflect research findings that parents whose children go on child protection registers have often asked for help and support without getting it, on a number of occasions in the year before the registration (Dalgaard 1991).

Many of the priorities identified by parents would alleviate the difficulties described by these parents, and might prevent them and others reaching crisis point or being unable to continue to cope with their children's needs.

Information needs

One of the views frequently aired in the local media and in discussions about residents in Wood End, Henley Green and Bell Green, is that they are 'apathetic', 'not interested' or 'don't want to know'. The experience of talking to parents demonstrated that local residents were keen to have more information on a wide cross section of topics. Most of the issues raised in this section came from joint 'Drop In' sessions with the Save the Children Fund development worker, working with the Family Project. Many of these issues were echoed by other parents involved with the Henley Project. The 'Drop In' sessions were organised as part of the work for the Henley project. The development worker acted as coworker at the Family Project, offering general support and advice. The parents involved chose topics and issues which they wanted to know more about. These included:

Benefits and tax

* maintenance payments   - are there deductions from benefits?
                         - should payments be made whether man
                           working or not?
* social fund - grants and loans - how do you get them; who gets them
               - why do you have to wait six months when claiming on
                 your own for a budgeting loan
* income support - how is it worked out
                 - who/how do they decide what you need to live on
* child benefit/lone parent benefit/loss of income support
* how is Income Tax worked out?

Health

* ways to deal with symptoms/preventive measures - diabetes
                                                 - angina
                                                 - cystic fibrosis
                                                 - asthma
* how to treat childhood illnesses
* information about the local Women's Health and Information Centre
* why is hospital food so expensive- for visitors

- when staying over with your children
- waiting lists - how are decisions made about where people are on them
- diagnosis - should be in English not Latin — information is given on what it is, but not on prevention/treatment

Local authorities

- how is money allocated — and why — by central government to local authorities?
- was the police 'surgery' still giving advice to residents?
- what happened to the local Task Team's enquiries in the area?

Housing

- rent arrears/moving/transfers: how are decisions made; — appearance of different decisions being made for different people
- boarded up houses — why are there so many?
- what is the council's policy on homelessness?
- repairs
- roles of different housing officers — locally and citywide

Environmental services

- who is responsible for street cleaning services and clearing up rubbish?
- what happened to the Bottle Bank?

Social services

- what is their role?
- Children Act? — what is it, what difference will it make?
- policies on nurseries.

Education services

- their policies — generally: how to keep up with their children's education
- nurseries
- adult education courses

Children's safety equipment

- where to find it; which locking cabinets, stairgates etc., are safest
- why is safety equipment so expensive? — why does it have VAT — not a luxury, item it's essential

• Safe as Houses — what services do they offer? (Safe as Houses is a local voluntary sector project that people had heard of but didn't know what they did).

Gas service

• why have there been changes in standing charges — it is more expensive
• different methods of payment
• why was £5 the minimum payment in post offices?

> Locally you can pay using a payment book at the Post Office, but the minimum payment is £5. You can buy as little or as much as you like on a machine which is in the city centre. Why can't we buy less than £5's worth of gas locally?

The Drop In was not set up specifically to look at issues of concern to parents about their children. However during the period the development worker worked with this group, most of the discussions and debates centred on this theme. Not only did parents want information but they were also great sources of information about current issues that affected their own and their children's lives. The two way flow of information between the Henley Safe Children Project development worker and the parents from the Drop In provided the Project with valuable information about the area and access to a wide cross section of people with different interests and priorities. It also ensured widespread sharing of information and mutual support between many different local projects and groups.

This range of information and concerns demonstrates parents' commitment to try to understand how a wide range of policies and decisions affect them and their children. It also demonstrates the energy and interest which groups of people can bring to improving their own and others' situations.

Child care and protection

Groups of Drop In parents also asked to know more about the prevention of sexual abuse of children. They watched the Puppet Gang Video and had discussions about the issues this raised. They and many other mothers involved with the Henley Project wanted to have more information on child protection issues. Their questions included:

> If you are on the Child Protection Register would you know?
> What support generally is there for parents, from anywhere? You only get it when the children have been harmed.
> What are parents' rights?
> What is considered child abuse?

A group of parents were made very angry about the lack of media attention to the dangers of sexual offenders 'grooming' young children, sometimes by making friends with and being helpful to their parents. They wanted much more emphasis to be placed on this in the media and in schools. This followed a presentation which parents gave at an NSPCC conference, where they heard a paper about the behaviour of offenders. This made them realise that attention was given by themselves and schools to 'stranger danger' far more than danger from known adults, yet statistics showed that children were most likely to be abused by men known to them.

Two parents' groups asked the worker to provide information on what is considered child abuse. Before they looked at official definitions of abuse the group wrote their own list. Although the parents did not feel that they knew what would be considered child abuse, they still came up with definitions of abuse remarkably similar to the official ones. Some of these parents were later involved in advising a local authority worker who was given responsibility for developing information leaflets.

Parents whose children were in care or supervised by Social Services said:

We don't know what our rights are, we should know.

We have found that talking to people doesn't work, we need to put things in writing.

They did not think that they were well enough informed about, or involved in planning for their children's future well being.

Parents' priorities

When asked what they thought would help to support them in keeping their children safe, parents involved with the Drop In sessions identified the following priorities:

We want a park, maintained and cleaned by the council.

Play areas that you can go to with children, especially young children:
- away from roads
- no dogs
- fenced in
- supervised by parents
- benches for parents
- larger lawned areas
- nice safe climbing frame.

We want a special bus service, for families.

Safety on the street for children from cars — we need zebra crossings — more speed ramps in the road.

We want our kids to be healthy, not have sickness and diarrhoea.

We don't want so many dogs on the estate, should people be allowed only one dog each?

We want to see if we can get something done for Monkswood, for example, play equipment. (Monkswood has local reputation as being a particularly difficult area).

We want to keep Monkswood clean, especially from dog's mess and breaking plastic bags of rubbish.

Other small scale areas were also identified by their residents as needing special initiatives.

We want a really good clear up, regularly, to get rid of:
* animal mess
* car and motorbike bits
* glass
* dirty nappies
* stray dogs.

Two parents, when talking about providing activities for older children, said that it should be remembered:

that a lot of children don't like taking part in sport and that perhaps other activities with a constructive purpose beside sport should be considered.

One parent made the point that:

It is your responsibility to keep your children safe, what about other people's responsibilities to me and my family's safety — for example the Housing Department, I have to live with shale and my windows falling out?

There had been many problems because of poor construction throughout the life of this 1950's estate. Some groups thought that the policy of allocating flats to parents with young children should be changed.

From working in the Drop In it was clear to the worker that parents were anxious to discuss problems, difficulties and issues as they came up, rather than having to wait for appointments or even to be put on waiting lists. It appeared that in some instances having the opportunity to share their concerns, worries and experiences with other parents was all that they needed.

Overall, there was a sense of determination to try to provide the best possible opportunities for their children, but many individual parents expressed frustration and sometimes depression about how hard it was to give their children what they thought they needed. They wanted a cleaner, safer environment, easier access to family support services and childcare, better health care and education.

Summary of parents' priorities

There were many recurring themes. The frequency with which particular concerns and priorities were raised throughout all the groups is summarised below:

Over two thirds mentioned

park/safe play area;

More than half mentioned

safety on the street generally for children;
safety on the street from other children;
supervised activities for children (included holiday and after school care);
preschool childcare provision — creches to support activities (for example, employment and training);
problem of asking for help and not getting it;

A third to half mentioned

some form of accessible community transport;
respite care for parents with young children;
independent support/counselling for parents;
need for more information on what is available;
need for information on children's and parent's rights;
safety on streets for children from cars/bikes;
clean up — keeping areas clean;
feeling free from intimidation; ·

Over a fifth mentioned

problems for families in flats with children;
more information on services, roles of different workers in child protection;
children being drawn into crime on the streets;
need for baby sitting services;
concerns about young children being on the street at inappropriate times;
racial harassment on the street and at home (including encouraging children to shout and give racist abuse);
negative and insensitive attitudes of some police;
problems with stray dogs;

Other things mentioned

dealing with some children's irresponsible actions;
need for:
• work with employers to encourage holiday provisions for children —
  job share policies;
• milk at schools infants and juniors;
• holidays for parents, on their own and with their children;
• support for men;
parents worried about making friends;
parents worried about their children's friends parents: for example are
  they in the house, taking drugs etc.
conflicting advice from professionals;
harassment of children who are disabled or have a learning disability;
better public transport;
child friendly facilities at Doctors/Hospitals/Shops;
fear of child protection services;
phones not working;
lack of fences and gates on gardens;
not getting the local Community newsletter;
training and support on being a parent;
making use of resources outside of the area, for example OSABA;
not being able to move out of the area once you've moved into it;
better information on the health needs of minority ethnic groups;
need to give young people a positive outlook on life.

The comments and views of parents involved in the Henley Safe
Children Project reflected the views of parents and workers collected
during the Under 8s Review, organised as part of the implementation of
the Children Act 1989. The results of this local forum, as well as results
from other parts of the city, showed concerns similar to those of Henley
Safe Children parents, and were echoed by workers throughout the city.
They are very similar to concerns and problems identified by parents in
a Bristol study (Gill 1992).

The local Wood End, Bell Green and Henley Green Forum discussed the availability, cost and quality of creches. There were concerns
that voluntary organisations did not have access to funds to provide
creches, especially to meet new Children Act 1989 requirements.
Generally it was felt that there needed to be a range of childcare facilities
available to parents to meet different needs — such as respite or emergency care; creches to support parents attending activities; playschemes
and after school care. The lack of commitment to funding for and access
to childcare services generally was a key concern.

It was also stressed that many parents and workers did not have
access to adequate information about the resources, facilities, and
services that were already available.

Many individuals and groups identified the need for support groups, educational/parenting groups for parents with children, both young children and older children. The need for readily available counselling for adults and children was stressed.

Lack of suitable, available and affordable transport for parents and children to help get to activities, medical appointments and to do shopping was mentioned by many.

Parents and workers alike highlighted the need for safe play areas for children of all ages, especially 5-8 year olds, as this would help prevent young children being drawn into petty crime. A need to provide constructive activities and encourage socially responsible behaviour of young people was identified. The behaviour on the streets of older children and young people was seen as a problem. Although crime was mainly committed by males, some of the women involved with the project thought that young women often played a part in crime and antisocial behaviour, and attention was needed to their behaviour as well as that of boys and young men.

In the area of the project, where there were two parents involved in the care of a family, many of these families had financial problems. Unemployment was common. Some fathers worked outside Coventry. However the main information for the project came from women, who generally saw themselves as the main carers — many of them caring alone, or with previous experience of caring alone. The relentless practicalities of caring for young children were generally tackled by these women with ingenuity, good humour and dedication. Local women particularly showed energy and optimism throughout the project, in spite of the pressures and difficulties they faced in bringing up children in an area of disadvantage. There were few opportunities for movement into more comfortable life styles for them and their children, yet much of their energy and commitment went into providing the best start in life possible for their children.

In the local forum, in other groups throughout the city who were consulted about services for families with children, as well as in the Henley Safe Children Project, parents wanted much greater priority to be given to services which would improve the quality of life and opportunities for young children. They wanted Social Services too provide more childcare for all under 5s — not just 'priority' children. They wanted after school clubs and activities, youth clubs and playschemes to be provided, in partnership, with education, community education and leisure services.

Overall, the need for better opportunities for all age groups — children and adults — well co-ordinated, was a key theme.

Many of these groups stressed the importance of paying attention to issues of gender, race and disability in the development of services for young children. Other issues of equal opportunities were raised such as the lack of information available in translation; buildings which were inaccessible to people in wheelchairs.

There was a very substantial consensus between local people and workers about the improvements needed. The next chapter will focus on the views of local workers.

Continuing work by parents

One group of mothers — up to 8 in all — met regularly throughout the project. They spent time discussing in more detail what they felt they needed to help support them in bringing up their children in Wood End. They also talked to agencies about what they would like to see happen in the future.

The group met with the Area Management Team (AMT), members from Leisure Services and the Parks Department to give their views on the need for local play areas, as well as to hear what proposals there were for any new work in the area. They also completed a questionnaire which the Parks Department sent out on what they would want from a Park, and sent a written response to the Community Parks Policy Consultation Document.

They met on a number of occasions with the Area Co-ordinator to discuss the progress of the AMT's work. They shared with the coordinator their feelings about some of the negative experiences of past consultation exercises held in the area as well as pointing out some of the issues which they felt needed tackling. They emphasised:

> In the past we've been asked for information or surveyed for our views and what we would like to see happen. We have *not* been properly consulted about living in the area. However, through the Henley Safe Children Project, we have had the opportunity to express out feelings, views and fears and to see these written down and valued by key agencies involved in child protection.

Members of this group acted as local representatives on a number of planning, strategy and advisory groups. The group met with a local health manager to find out more about the structures of the Health Service and the Patients' Charter. This meeting resulted in the group sending letters to the Family Health Service Authority, the Community Health Council, information officers of the local hospitals, asking them to outline their policies on providing child-friendly facilities at GP's surgeries, clinics and hospitals.

They arranged a meeting with representatives of a Community Nursery to find out how they had set up a community nursery in another area of Coventry.

The group prepared the following notes on services they wanted to see provided, and who they should approach to discuss them with.

Child care provision

Need to talk to:

Social Services
Councillors
Organisations that have available childcare space

About:

- slots during the week where you can leave children to do shopping etc.
  This would be time limited — short time — and it would need to take into account
  - special needs of different children
  - different ages
  - cost — look at community nurseries and possibility of subsidised places
  - possibilities for a playscheme
  - that people do not earn enough money in the area to pay childminders

Youth services and activities

Need to talk to:

Community Education
Family Project

About:

- more places for care activities for older children 7-11, 11-18, nearer home
- involving young people in consultations about their experience of living in the area.

Need to talk to:

Youth Services

About:

- boys groups as well as girls groups;
- the fact that clubs have been closed; now only one at Potters Green;
- outreach worker with young people

Employment opportunities

Need to talk to:

Employment Development Project

About:

- training opportunities eg. counselling; office skills; creche work;
- cheap transport, a community bus/taxi with a driver

Traffic dangers

Need to talk to:

Police
Local Authority

About:

- zebra crossings
- more traffic bumps and other safety measures in particular localities

Street safety

Need to talk to:

Community Safety Officer
Police
NSPCC
Probation

About:

- safety on the streets for children
- other people's children's irresponsible actions
- behaviour of young people
- police handling of reports from local residents: remembering not to identify publicly those who report crime

The group also prepared their own leaflet, setting out some of the area's needs.

As a result of some of the discussions that were held with agencies and workers, parents in this group realised that often they had the same concerns as professionals — one mother summed up their view:

We live with these statistics everyday as residents in Wood End. The other thing we live with is the fact that people assume that we don't care about our children. We do have the *same* fears as professionals for our children — we also have the same expectations for them as everyone else does.

They also raised the following points:

Through the work we have done we have found that people do care but we need support to carry on caring. Barriers to help us to care need to be removed, for example meetings to be held in school hours, creches to be provided, meeting places to be local or transport to be provided. We want to help professionals to help us.

Families do chose to live in Wood End, because of this we want to improve the whole way of life for families who live in the area now and for generations to come.

We all have a responsibility to make children safe!

4 Views of paid workers in the neighbourhood

Meetings and discussions were held with a wide range of workers from voluntary and statutory agencies in the area, about their views on the needs of parents and children. There were informal meetings with individuals from a cross section of local agencies, statutory and voluntary; some were arranged as part of the development worker's induction process, some were part of ongoing collaborative work on particular issues and projects. There were also discussions and meetings where workers were asking for information and advice from the development worker. More formal meetings also included interagency networks and groups e.g. the Henley Safe Children Project Steering Group, the local interdepartmental Family Support Group, Social Services Under 5s Managers, Community Education, Social Services. Other local childcare workers, advice centre workers, employment and women's training networks, volunteers and workers from voluntary agencies were involved in the informal and formal groups.

This chapter gives an account of the main issues and themes identified during the meetings. These were recorded under the following headings:

- Income
- Housing and local facilities
- Services
- Communication
- Parent's needs
- Children's needs
- Child protection issues
- Discrimination and oppression; equal opportunities

Inadequate income

Low income was seen as a major problem for large numbers of individuals and families in the area. Single parents — usually mothers — were a particular source of concern — described by workers as being caught in a poverty trap which brought long term problems. Loss of benefits and inability to find or pay for childcare provided major obstacles to any return to work.

Charities were seen as crucial at times to helping some families, but some workers were concerned that schools and Social Services used them largely for 'crisis' help to individuals, rather than as part of a supportive project which might have wider benefits. They were anxious to see more strategic approaches developed (see Blackburn 1992). As an example, a local charity set up a used clothing shop during the course of the project. After hearing about the frequent use of charitable trusts the project worker raised questions with a number of agencies about possible benefits in monitoring the number of charitable applications made from the area. This would provide an opportunity to work in a more coordinated way, possibly showing ways in which limited funds could be more effectively used. There were initiatives locally to set up a credit union.

Food parcels were sometimes given to families by the local nursery, particularly when Giros had been lost. Secondhand clothing from jumble sales was commonly relied on by many families.

'Informal' prostitution by girls and young women was thought by some workers to be one response to inadequate income.

Debt and inadequate income provided a familiar context in discussions with local workers. Feelings of powerlessness and inadequacy — in being unable to provide adequate supports in these circumstances — were regularly expressed. They represented a continuing theme in Steering Group Meetings.

Housing and local facilities

Although there had been substantial improvements to housing in many parts of the area, not all areas had benefited. A recent major refurbishment had included putting up fences and gates to provide houses with their own front gardens; painting the rendering on the outside of the houses; new window frames and door frames; either a new kitchen or bathroom; knocking down old medium rise blocks of flats or refurbishing them. The local authority had provided substantial funding for upgrading the parts of the estate which were hardest to let and had collaborated with a Housing Association to develop a range of tenancy schemes and sales.

A common view was that these improvements were long overdue. However some workers (and parents) did state that 'improving the outside of the houses is good but does not change what is going on inside them'. The context for this comment was a discussion about the difficulties people were experiencing living their day to day lives, for example lack of money, difficulties with childcare, relationship problems. Making the outside of people's houses look good did not make these things go away. Some workers questioned whether the money would be better spent on supporting families day to day. Like the parents, they were raising issues about strategic planning, to recognise the interconnectedness of problems.

Most workers and parents understood that the money was only available for refurbishment and thought it was a great improvement. Cynicism, however, based on past experiences of local authority attempts to sort out Wood End's problems in particular, influenced people's view about why this *face lift* of houses was being done, when they could not see people's real day to day lives changing.

Leisure opportunities and safe constructive play spaces were identified as major gaps in the area's facilities There was concern expressed about the resources, safety, conditions and management of the local adventure playground. Workers were not satisfied with the extent to which local parents were able to be involved. A problem of lack of suitable premises for creches and other childcare facilities and community activities was identified. Many buildings available were too small and cramped, badly heated and poorly decorated

A number of workers said they would have liked school buildings to be used more extensively, but thought that fear of destruction of property was one of the factors which prevented this. The staffing costs at a time of cuts were also seen as a major barrier.

Services

The need for services to be better coordinated and to relate more closely to what is known about levels of deprivation in the area was identified by many workers, in both statutory and voluntary agencies. Information, which would be readily accessible to residents and workers in the area, about different services available, changes in provision (e.g. the reorganisation of community education services) was said to be needed. A 'one stop shop' was suggested as a partial solution. A wide range of information for workers, children and parents and a focus for consultation and sharing could be further developed from such a base. The work of the local authority Area Management Team, set up after the Henley Project began, tied in closely with this perspective. The team worked with local groups and agencies to increase the flow of information and to increase opportunities for consultation and partnership.

Another focus for consultation, sharing and self help development was the Wood End Family Project, set up, at the same time as the Henley Project started, just before the Area Management Team (AMT). It had been set up as a result of local workers and residents identifying needs for family support which were not being met by mainstream services. There was something of an irony in two largely separate initiatives with the same concerns — The Henley Safe Children Project and the Wood End Family Project — being set up at the same time. Different groups and agencies had been involved in planning and fundraising, but fortunately came together closely at the point where they both obtained funding and they worked in close collaboration. Their work was complementary, as the Henley Project was short term, concerned with gathering information about child protection and family support needs and committed to facilitate parents' involvement with agencies in planning to meet them. The Wood End Family Project sought money for a purpose built centre, where a wide range of supportive activities could be housed. The building was funded by a capital grant through the Urban

Programme. Other revenue grants from the Urban Programme, Church Urban Fund, Children in Need etc., funded a childcare worker, administration and caretaking work as well as running costs. Save the Children Fund employed the development worker. The Project developed a wide range of participative schemes in response to residents' stated needs, for example, the 'Drop In' sessions and 'Allsorts Support Group', a parents and toddlers group, a community launderette, as well as opportunities for volunteering within the project.

Workers supported the idea of better coordination of such work, and showed commitment to working more closely in partnership with each other, even though many expressed feelings of great frustration at the demands already on them, particularly from constant reorganisation. There was frequent staff turnover. Many expressed a sense of being dominated by crisis responses and short term fragmented work.

The Area Management Team sponsored a Family Support Group, drawing representatives from a cross section of statutory and voluntary agencies e.g. community education, social services, health, a mediation project, a local City Mission, the Wood End Family Project and Henley Safe Children Project as well as local parents. This group considered in detail neighbourhood needs and drew up proposals for a coordinated Family Support Strategy.

The need for much more extensive childcare provision, child friendly services and supportive services for parents with young children was stressed by many workers. Increased support for extended family networks was thought to be needed, so that they could more easily be involved in caring for children. One local headmaster stated that:

> There are lots of people who need to use services, but it is much more difficult to manage if you have any other children with you. Lots of people need support and cannot get it because they cannot arrange to get there.

Greater involvement of parents in planning childcare services was thought important by some workers — the Under 8s Review under the Children Act was given as an example of where it would have been beneficial to have much greater consultation and involvement. There was wide support for the idea that all agencies should be involved in planning preventive services.

Workers thought that particular gaps had been left by cuts or losses in the following:
- city farm — near a local Family Centre
- parents' support group run at a Neighbourhood Centre
- job/career sessions run from an Adventure Playground
- Adult Literacy/Community Education Worker being absorbed back into teaching staff at a school (Burnham Post)
- a number of creches
- the local Advice Centre being expected to cover a wider area with the same resources

- Schools' parent link workers — 'lollipop' workers and tuck shop helpers now had added responsibilities of linking with parents
- Child Guidance services
- Home/School Counsellor at one of the schools — used to run parents' group
- courses for parents with special educational needs
- Voluntary Help Organiser post
- Section 11 money was no longer available to promote better services for minority ethnic groups
- Social Services coordination of a fieldworkers' forum
- a common view was that increasing paperwork and bureaucracy in Social Services and Health, without extra resources, meant less face to face work with users of services.

Communication

A recurring theme in discussions with local workers was the inadequacy of current ways of spreading information about services and about expectations and responsibilities of agencies, both statutory and voluntary. Formal methods of information giving — through letters, leaflets, council sponsored papers, and the local paper: Bush Telegraph — although needed, were in many cases thought to be less effective than face to face discussions, spreading information through people's natural networks. Such informal methods were acknowledged to be very time consuming. However some workers believed there were additional problems about using these methods because some agencies had insufficient understanding of and commitment to:

- community development methods
- providing the resources needed to remove practical barriers to access and consultation
- dealing with the issue of power when attempts were made to involve or consult residents
- tapping into local experiences and skill in how to talk to and listen to local residents
- the timescales involved in building up trust and effective communication
- differences between workers and local people about what consultation means
- the importance of constraints on local people's time — such as commitments in childcare, transport problems
- recognising when information could only be gained from agencies or places which would stigmatise them or cause embarrassment if they were seen there.

Workers identified the need for a shift in local culture amongst paid workers and residents, which would acknowledge past histories in some agencies, where clients felt devalued, felt they were not being listened to, did not believe that services would be accessible to them. A number of workers said that agencies needed to recognise that simply providing a service did not ensure accessibility.

More workers needed to recognise that sometimes parents only got heard if they were awkward, or fighters. This should be seen as a strength, a demonstration of commitment to their children's needs, for example, rather than evidence of lack of cooperation. Unrealistic attitudes, critical judgments of why some local people behaved the way they did needed challenging.

Some of the local authority support and advice services were much less well known or recognised by local people than their more formal responsibilities for education and child protection. Changes in provision of nursery places so that most families who used them were seen as at risk or vulnerable meant an increasing suspicion and anxiety about the Social Services department.

The skills of local people in communicating effectively with agencies were recognised. One example given of this was a proposal by the council to put a rubbish tip at the back of Wood End housing estate. Local residents let councillors know, in no uncertain terms, that they didn't want the tip. Residents lobbied council meetings and sent in a petition objecting to the proposal. The proposal was dropped. Some workers thought that there was a need for more emphasis on sharing skills — amongst statutory and voluntary agencies and residents.

When there were street disturbances in the summer of 1992, local workers and residents showed their concern to do something about this by attending a public meeting. Yet the problems underlying the disturbances were well known to many people. Workers felt that this meeting showed the generally *reactive* response to local people and local needs, whereas what was needed was a coordinated, *proactive* approach. Again, this view fitted closely with the stated aims of the new Area Management Team, and parallels recent emphasis on strategic planning and the need for children's services plans (Baldwin and Spencer 1993; Audit Commission 1994; SSI/DoH 1996; Cannan and Warren 1997; Sinclair et al. 1997).

In several discussions the view was given that access to some resources had been missed because information about them had not been shared, for example, access to grants for equipment for Safe as Houses, a Voluntary Sector project which provides home and safety equipment such as stair gates, lockable cupboards etc.; and grants for childminding.

Some resources — behaviour management courses was given as an example — might have been used more effectively if they had been better coordinated. Workers described confusion about who should decide the need for such courses — agencies or parents; whether childcare was available to allow parents to attend, and about what should be the response to parents who repeated the course several times. These were seen as needed, valuable, resources which had not been used as cost-effectively as they might be. The under 5s Managers' Group agreed to work on these issues.

Some parts of the area were thought to get less attention than others — Henley Green was given as one example — which could lead local people to feel left out. Some workers felt that they did not generally have enough up to date background information about the area. One headmaster made this point when he referred to the usefulness of the Henley Safe Children Project's Interim Report, saying

> It gave a full and complete picture and covered all aspects. It was helpful to have the statistics to back up what you 'know' about it.

He thought that everyone working in the area would find it helpful to have this detailed information readily available.

Many local workers from a wide range of agencies were not happy about the extent to which they were consulted about the needs of the area when strategic plans were being drawn up. Many felt that they had not been listened to, or their views had been devalued. There were times when it was not clear which agency was responsible for dealing with a problem. Examples given included:

- domestic violence; is it a housing, health, police, social services issue?
- difficulties in bringing up children; is this a community education, education, social services, health, voluntary sector, police issue?
- fear of crime, intimidation; is this a police, social services, mediation project, probation, community education issue?

Workers raised questions about what happens if a family are experiencing all these difficulties: do the other agencies communicate about their roles and responsibilities? Not all agencies showed awareness of each other's services and resources. The lack of agreed geographical boundaries across all agencies was seen as a continuing problem — but one which was being tackled.

Workers had a lot of commitment to taking a more strategic approach to services for children and families, but often expressed frustration that many of their efforts seemed to achieve all too little. They recognised the need for multiagency and interagency approaches to policy and practice at grass roots, management and policy development levels.

Parents' needs and stresses

Low income, the stresses associated with it and low self esteem were thought by many workers to be associated with aggressive behaviour, lack of pride in themselves and in their environment. It was pointed out that many parents had no opportunities for time on their own. There were many single parents facing huge demands and stresses. Those in partnerships often had difficulties in their relationships. All groups drew attention to the range of difficulties and stresses they thought the majority of people in the area had to struggle with.

One worker expressed a concern that there was a substantial amount of 'informal prostitution' in the area. This same worker had a view that occasionally older women took up with teenage boys, getting a kick out of the flattering attention. She described her view of a shift in recent years from large numbers of 'downtrodden women in their 40s, in bad physical condition' but whose children were well cared for, to more parents who were well dressed and would be seen smoking and drinking, but their children might be in bad physical health, and be badly dressed. This attitude contrasted with that of many workers who described the ingenuity and dedication of many mothers in keeping their children well clothed, and putting their needs first.

Crime in the area was a source of stress to many. 'Loan Sharks' were also seen as a problem. A minister who had helped to start a Credit Union was said to have been burgled nine times.

Dependence on drugs such as valium and frequent use of marijuana were identified as problems for some parents.

Some workers expressed the view that some unwanted pregnancies and sometimes large families were related to distaste — by both men and women — for using physical methods of contraception and anxiety about oral contraceptives. Thus cuts in family planning services and their increasing inaccessibility were identified as exacerbating this problem. Teenage pregnancies were thought to be increasing and were seen as related to this. The particular stresses of young mothers were seen as warranting special attention by some health workers.

Workers associated difficulties parents experienced with young children and adolescents with lack of 'shared care' facilities such as after school activities, holiday care, support for family holidays, flexible childcare provision. Some workers believed that it was not uncommon for professional workers to disapprove of some childcare arrangements. They failed to understand the value to parents of time away from their children and how this could benefit children. Creches were seen by some as second class childcare and therefore to be avoided, rather than supported. The regulatory function of Social Services — particularly since the implementation of the Children Act — was seen by some as a barrier, rather than a support for childcare provision which would ease the burdens on parents. Some workers expressed the view that there were problems both in attitudes and in inadequate resources.

Differing views of how children's needs would best be met were reflected in discussions about the merit of encouraging mothers to spend time with their children versus the provision of creches which could provide practical help for them in meeting household responsibilities as well as having time for themselves. It was a measure of the generally low expectations about how much help parents could expect with childcare that these were discussed as though they were alternatives. In more affluent neighbourhoods mothers might be expected to have easier access to both types of opportunity — substitute care and quality time with their children.

Local support networks were recognised as important to parents — often people with local knowledge and links took on 'aunt and uncle' roles. Workers described how frequently parents supported each other through exchanging clothes, looking after each other's children, providing a sympathetic ear.

Workers noted a lack of information available to parents about domestic violence and child abuse. Domestic violence was thought to be much more common than local statistics suggested. There was thought to be a particular lack of information about sexual abuse. This was confirmed by a group of parents who attended an NSPCC Seminar to talk about their experiences of living in Wood End, and were angry to hear about the extent of child molestation by people in caring roles who 'groomed' children before abusing them. They believed that too little emphasis was given to this in the 'stranger danger' approach often used in the media. Workers also thought that parents needed more information about the effects of sexual abuse; about dangers from babysitters; about contacts with and protection from those convicted of sexual offences in the past. Involvement of parents in identifying needs and planning responses was seen as important by most workers. Few felt satisfied with current arrangements and skills and opportunities available to ensure that this happened.

Children's needs and child protection issues

In addition to the issues raised in the section above, mainly relating to parents' needs, workers identified numerous concerns about children's needs and the protection of children.

Workers from agencies not involved in statutory child protection, for example the Advice Centre and the Outreach Project, said that they felt they were now having to work with people who could not get Social Services help, because it was only available in crisis situations or following a formal child protection investigation. Some of the families they were working with had child protection problems. Linked to this, other workers outside statutory child protection agencies mentioned the difficulty they had getting training on child protection issues and procedures, as well as information on the Children Act and its implications.

Some workers expressed particular concern about the behaviour of some local children: unruly children, children who either have no self-discipline, who may break things or get angry or frustrated or are frozen, blank or withdrawn. Some said that there was a lot of emotional abuse and deprivation, as well as verbal abuse towards children. They talked of children craving affection. One worker described an incident where a mother greeted her children at school by kicking them.

There was knowledge of children unsupervised in the street who were too young to be on their own; knowledge of children left alone at home, or caring for younger children in unsafe circumstances. There was an acknowledgement by some workers that it would be quite impossible for social workers to investigate every situation where there was concern, and that in an area with the acute problems of some parts of the ward, it was inevitable that there would be an acceptance of some undesirable situations as 'normal'. However many workers identified families with such severe problems and worries about their children's behaviour, that they feared a downward spiral leading to risks of serious harm. They did not feel that the urgency of children's needs in the area was matched by the resources and support services currently available.

The investigations for child abuse, as well as matching the areas of most severe deprivation, were also very common in the areas closest to social services offices and provision. We do not have enough information about this to draw conclusions as to whether it connected with a greater readiness of local people to report concerns when they are close to such facilities. The range of people referring was as wide as in other areas.

Many workers' concerns about meeting children's needs were similar to those outlined by parents in the previous section. They particularly highlighted the lack of services to help children directly. Workers also stressed that children needed free, independent counselling services that were available immediately. The Henley Safe Children Project worker was approached on numerous occasions about the availability of free counselling services for children. There was no service available for these children or for young people, except through complicated referral processes in health, social services or education. There would usually be a very long waiting period for these services. Some were only available after investigation of abuse, or evidence of severe distress. Often it would be months after a referral that any help would be given.

Workers also identified the need for constructive activities and play schemes which provided meals and safe play areas for all age groups. These needed to take account of local attitudes. One worker mentioned that:

> Parents have identified that it is sometimes difficult to motivate children to join groups and activities due to peer pressure or when it is located at school: children may often have negative attitudes to school.

Another worker also questioned whether there needed to be

... a rethink of how workers play with children? They need to be with children in the streets rather than expect children to attend centres which have safer environments.

These provisions could more constructively be seen as complementary, than as alternatives. It was suggested that outreach work should be done with older children to ensure that a safer environment for younger children would be created.

Several workers stated that there was a need for more provision for older children and young people. They felt that increasing activities and services to meet children's and young people's needs would help to reduce boredom, glue sniffing, young children being drawn into petty crime. One worker stated:

Solvent sniffing is a big problem in the area and a lot of children are putting their lives at risk because of it.

Another expressed concern that:

The Community Drugs Team does not work with people under the age of 18. Some of the children involved in this area are as young as 8.

They also believed that a wider range of purposeful activities would help to reduce stresses on families and hence child abuse.

Children's educational needs were discussed. Workers talked about difficulties for children whose parents were unable to or did not support them at home — for example in help with reading. They thought that there was a need for much greater attention to educational needs of local children. Some wondered how many parents might like to become governors of schools but did not know how. Concerns about the loss of some services to children were also discussed, particularly a local school stopping its creche provision and reabsorbing a parent-school worker back into the teaching staff.

The lack of child friendly facilities, for example at doctors' surgeries and hospitals, was highlighted, as well as the general lack of child centred activities. A need was identified for a childcare coordinator, who would promote a more coherent range of childcare arrangements, and also have responsibility for creche provision.

Discrimination and oppression: equal opportunities

A perception among many of the local workers — as well as residents — was that few Black or Asian people live in the area and therefore 'race' was not an issue. A notable exception to this view was in nursery provision. The Social Services nurseries have Equal Opportunities Policy statements, which they make clear to parents through letters when they use the provision. Their displays, toys, books and meals also reflect the fact that Coventry is a multicultural city. The letter to parents states the nursery's commitment to equal opportunities and also clearly indicates that discriminatory behaviour will be challenged. Amongst some workers there was some understanding that it must be difficult for Black people to live in the area. Black groups and individuals involved with the Henley project were mainly contacted through a city wide group OSABA. Their views were in sharp contrast to that of many workers. They described the difficulties of local access to supportive services. The only local group which the project was able to obtain information from was a group run by Community Education for mothers of children of mixed racial heritage. In chapter two it was noted that use of services by Black residents was below what would have been expected, given their numbers in the area.

A few workers discussed the fact that there were almost no targeted services for Black or Asian people in the area. They said that there was a need for information generally to be translated, although there is also a lack of information on the translation needs of the area. It had not been possible to obtain adequate information about the languages of minority groups in the area for the Henley Project to arrange for appropriate translations at the beginning of the project.

Concerns were expressed as to whether special needs — learning difficulties and physical disabilities — of parents and of children, were being met locally. Access to many buildings — for adults and for children with disabilities — was identified as a problem. One worker claimed that parents whose children had disabilities had access to some resources, but that parents who were themselves disabled did not.

Workers raised many issues about gender when discussing children's and parents' needs. Some workers highlighted the fact that the majority of face to face workers across all statutory and voluntary agencies were women, whilst most of the managers were men. This was thought to affect the amount of attention given to timing of events, provision of childcare, creches and other issues of access. The lack of creche facilities at the local Employment Development Project was given as one example of the many barriers to women's participation in educational and employment opportunities.

Concern was expressed by a number of workers about the lack of positive male role models for many children under 5 — in their own homes and in childcare provision. It was extremely rare for males to be employed as nursery workers or creche workers. The exceptions were one local nursery teacher and a recently appointed male health visitor.

Several groups discussed the view that domestic violence and its impact on the lives of women and children did not appear to be given sufficient priority by local agencies. It was felt by many local workers that the issue was being ignored, and therefore the links between domestic violence and child abuse were not being explored fully. Other issues linked to domestic violence were discussed: that there are only 200 bed spaces for women in hostels out of 1600 beds in the city; concerns about the effect on children of staying in a hostel.

Male attitudes to women were discussed, especially linked to women's and children's safety generally. A number of workers had concerns about how many men expressed macho attitudes and how many women seemed downtrodden and lacking in self esteem.

Current media and political claims about teenagers deliberately getting pregnant to gain access to housing and income did not find favour with most workers in the area. However some did express concerns about the numbers of young women in the area who became pregnant, and the local conditions which might encourage this. Poor access to family planning advice and counselling, as well as general distaste among some people for using contraceptives were identified as problems. Equally the poor opportunities for education and work experience were seen as hindering young people's feelings of being able to exercise control over their lives.

One worker expressed the view that some teenagers who were encouraged to keep their babies woke up to their missed opportunities in their twenties and became resentful. Other workers identified a problem with the way a few young women saw their babies almost like dolls, or as property.

The expectation that child care was women's responsibility, and the low level of practical involvement of many fathers in day to day care of their children, was frequently discussed. Some workers thought their own working practices did nothing to challenge the attitudes which this showed, as they were far more likely to work with mothers than with fathers. A mixture of practical opportunities, social attitudes, resources — or lack of them — led to a complex situation which needed further attention.

It was an area of concern at the end of the Henley Safe Children Project, that we had attempted to engage with *parents*, but in reality it was generally *mothers* who sought out the project. We did not specifically target the views and opinions of fathers. The issue of men's involvement in childcare and responsibility for the safety of children was nevertheless a key focus of the work. We did not however succeed in raising the level of consciousness of problems associated with common attitudes and the current division of labour in child care to the extent which we believed was necessary. This applied to our work with professionals and with local residents. In a follow on project with Asian groups in the Midlands (see Atkar et al 1997) we chose to work separately with men and women — something which might have been helpful in the Henley project had we had sufficient resources.

There was a close correspondence between the views expressed by workers about the needs for family support in the area, those expressed by parents, and the findings of successful support projects. Three groups of workers involved in a formal consultation for the project summarised their views about priorities for improving family support and children's life chances in the area.

Group A

What is needed to support parents to bring up their children safely and well.
- Immediate response — more resources
- Right kinds of resources
- Trained counsellors for parents and children
- Support for all parents regardless of age of children
- Recognition that being a parent is very difficult — valuing parenting
- Early intervention
- Consistency of professional/voluntary workers
- Workers in area need support, valuing, networking
- Sharing information (inter/agency)
- Partnership with parents and agencies/providers
- Courses on:
  - Coping skills/confidence raising
  - Parenting skills — handling conflict
                coping with crises
                prioritising
                budgeting
                negotiating etc.
- Link with health visitors to promote what is available
- Very local, very informal opportunities
- Outreach work
- Access to shops with affordable fresh produce
- Work on drug abuse/dealing
- Confidence to complain, request services

Group B

Communication
- Pre-birth help
- Schools to include issues in their curriculum
- Awareness of issues
- Work on life-skills
- Awareness of what is/is not acceptable re abuse
- Agencies need to have credibility
- Awareness of purpose of agencies and what they can/cannot do
- Non-stigmatised access

Group C

What is needed to support parents in bringing up their children safely and well:
- MONEY!! To fund resources, facilitators

- Outreach workers for all ages
- More information available to parents
- Self help groups — e.g. parents and toddlers
- Agency interaction
- Information sharing — to allay parental fears, and fear of being watched/observed (when people are identified as being involved with the Henley Safe Children Project some parents that they know, fear that their children are being watched/observed by them and they keep away. However other parents have come to Henley Safe Children Project members for information, advice and support)
- Local work to allay fear of social services
- Positive initiatives to handle peer pressure and labelling (negative views from neighbours etc.)
- A need for positive publicity
- More attention at grass roots level given by people actually living in the area
- Women's groups/parents groups
- Initial support — ice breakers — help to break in a group
- Catalyst
- Combating isolation
- Fear of getting too close to neighbours — cannot always trust them
- Health visitors have 'a foot in the door' — could be used more positively
- Acceptable support systems with time (from workers or volunteers)
- Good relationships are paramount
- People who have time are the parents
- Balance between: knowledge
                   skills
                   experience
                   time
                   confidentiality
- Parents in the area understand the problems of other parents in the area
- Supervision of play areas by local people
- Recognising people's fears for their children
- Desperate people relating to desperate situations — helplessness — more money is needed to correct situation
- Correcting antisocial behaviour — being clear about who does the damage — instilling in children right from wrong — interpreting values — working to repair basic common values.

These priorities were closely reflected in the family support strategy which was developed during the life of the project, by statutory and voluntary workers and local parents, who formed the Family Support

Group responsible to the Area Management Team. This group applied for funding from numerous sources to develop the resources and partnership principles identified. Some of the detail of these plans will be discussed in the final chapter.

5 Community development work and prevention: process and issues

The Henley Project was planned as a partnership in prevention: to work with local people to identify what parents needed to bring up children in health and safety and to explore ways of improving opportunities for needs to be met.

It sought to follow principles outlined in Chapter 1 — in the account of projects which have been successful in improving conditions for children and families. It drew on traditional community development models, starting from an assumption that a partnership of local people with paid workers from voluntary and statutory agencies and groups was most likely to ensure effective use of expertise, skill, resources and commitment (Gulbenkian 1983; Beresford and Croft 1986; Craig and Mayo 1994; Mayo 1995; Henderson 1995; Cannan and Warren 1997). The partnership aims of the 1989 Children Act were central to the work. The project had a particular interest in exploring the implications of section 17 of the Children Act, which sets out the duty of local authorities to safeguard and promote the welfare of children in their area who are in need. The values on which the project was based — promoting the rights and wellbeing of all children, redressing disadvantage and inequalities of opportunity — demanded close collaboration with a wide range of agencies, groups, parents and young people in investigating and attempting to meet needs through a varied range of services and activities.

This chapter describes the ways in which the work of the project was developed and explores the processes involved in working with parents and groups in the area. It gives some of the views of parents and workers about the importance of paying attention to processes of working and to people's experience in attempting to meet needs. Issues for agencies, workers and local people in working together to improve the social environment and life chances of families and children are considered.

Processes of participation and ownership

The development worker drew on key participation points from the Sunderland T.A.C.T. project (Appendix 1) in beginning to explore ideas and bring local residents and workers together. She worked with the following assumptions:

1) Local people are experts about their neighbourhoods — they live there.
2) People want to be part of a caring community but there is a limit to the amount of care any community can offer — depending on the burdens that community already shoulders, and the resources made available to support and enable members of the community in their caring role.
3) Participation does not just happen — it must be worked at. This means using the right settings, providing the right facilities, eg. transport, childcare and using a style which allows participation.

'Involving the community' is an ongoing, long term process

4) We need to recognise skills, understanding and expertise wherever it lies, irrespective of a person's 'status'.
5) People must be involved in creating the solutions to the problems which they face.
6) Successful work will build on strengths.
7) Local people must share ownership of policies in the area.
8) Local experience of 'the system' can be a barrier to participation.
9) Language can be a barrier, for example, inadequate provision of interpreters and translations to facilitate use of services and to ensure full consultation with minority groups or use of professional jargon.

These assumptions led us to give as much attention to the way we worked as to the issues we explored and the content of the material we collected.

There was commitment to the principle that all parents, regardless of their sex, race, colour, religion, disability, ethnic or national origin, age, sexual orientation, marital status or social class, should feel encouraged and enabled to take part.

This meant taking specific steps to try to ensure barriers to access to the project would be removed — for example, for parents from minority ethnic communities and parents with children with disabilities or learning difficulties, as well as parents themselves with disabilities or learning difficulties. As we had anticipated, in a mainly white neighbourhood, with a white development worker responsible to white organisations, it took a great deal of time to make contact with Black groups. Work with Black groups and with groups working with children and parents with disabilities was still developing at the end of the project. We did not think it appropriate to intrude on individuals' privacy by asking questions about sexuality, marital status or social class, but made efforts to give a clear message in our literature and in our meetings that we were supportive and respectful of different household and family forms.

The values and principles on which the project was based demanded a long term commitment to work alongside people in the local community, to involve them fully in decisions about the way information would be used and what future work would be done. There are major issues of power in trying to work in partnership which need to be honestly acknowledged and worked on. Even in a small scale voluntary project the power of professional workers to influence events, to dictate the agenda, to use only the information which they see as important, is very great.

We emphasised the following points throughout the project, with local people and workers and with the major agencies supporting the project.

- Long time scales are needed: for detailed negotiation and re-negotiation of aims, priorities, working methods.
- Partnership cannot be token: respect is essential for the expertise of those whose health and welfare is under discussion.
- Structures of service delivery, use of resources, decision making, need to reflect partnership principles — involve members of the communities affected.
- Conflicts of interest need to be acknowledged.
- When constraints mean that needs cannot be met, or that other services must have priority, respect demands effective communication, information, follow up, for those affected.
- There is a need to ensure that equal opportunities for workers are matched by equal opportunities in services, which means giving priority to process as well as content, for example in timing, translations, ease of access, style of operation.

Ensuring that all relevant people have the opportunity to give their views and be involved in the development of a project can only be an aim. Neighbourhood, professional and interpersonal dynamics, practical constraints, inevitably mean that the ideal of full participation will be unattainable. However, if more than token involvement of local people was to be achieved, detailed attention over a lengthy period was needed to ensure that opportunities and structures were created to foster participation. This 'behind the scenes' work took up the bulk of the development worker's time. She spent an intensive induction period familiarising herself with the neighbourhood, reading around the subject, meeting local groups, before planning the most effective ways of developing the project work.

The links between principles of community development work and of feminist research — trying to give attention to the process, to reflect on ethical and political issues, to acknowledge power relations — were very clear to us (Roberts 1981; Bell and Roberts 1984; Graham and Jones 1992; Maynard and Purvis 1994), as was the complexity of trying to follow these principles in practice.

The aim of the project, to give local people a voice, to act as a catalyst for change with local people and agencies involved in child care, meant that action research and qualitative methods of information gathering were seen as more appropriate than extensive survey research. We were open about our concern that preventive work in child protection was being given insufficient priority and about our commitment to bring about change — to promote family support and action and services which would protect children and promote their wellbeing. Our intention was to engage in dialogue with parents in the locality about their experience of trying to bring up their children in health and safety. We wanted to make their voices heard by those who might have some power to change situations, as well as to stand alongside them in increasing their own expertise and power. To do this we tried to make our thinking accessible to participants, to use the information we were gathering with them in extensive dissemination, so that their analysis and understanding could develop alongside ours (Freire 1970 and 1972; Glucksmann 1994).

One development worker could not hope to gather in depth information from more than a small sample of parents and workers. There could be no guarantee that those who gave their views would be representative. The problem which most neighbourhood workers have of getting in contact with the most isolated and needy groups was acknowledged. The worker did however have access to many local groups who were interested in the same issues, particularly groups looking at the implementation of the 1989 Children Act; voluntary agencies and local people setting up a Family Centre; support and self help groups in the area. All these gave valuable information and put a wide range of parents in contact with the worker. In return she worked closely with these groups to take further some of their priorities and to develop an overview of the needs of children and families within the area. We do not claim that the material we have gathered gives a full or representative picture of the area or of all families within it. However we believe that its range and depth give it validity and illuminate the experience of many families and children.

There were three main stages in the project:

- Induction; planning and development work.
- Gathering information; extensive liaison and networking with groups trying to develop family support.
- Dissemination of the project's findings; evaluation with parents; work with voluntary and statutory groups to develop strategies of family support.

The combination of action research and development work, in partnership with local groups, demanded careful attention to flexible approaches and responses, a willingness to seize opportunities which offered themselves, respect for the priorities, interests and practical constraints of those we were working with. This did not readily lend itself to following an orderly planned timetable. There was substantial overlap between the different phases of the project. Work begun during it, is being continued in many ways: through some of the local groups we worked with; through the New Links Project supported by the NSPCC and through the Asian Children and Families Project of the NSPCC and Warwick University (Atkar et al 1997).

Groups and individuals participating in the Henley Project

Eleven groups met in the main work of the project, to document their views. Ten were local to the project area; one included parents from other areas of the city who were meeting to discuss child protection concerns. One of these groups was known to involve a parent who had a child with special needs. Only one of the groups included people from minority ethnic communities — an Asian grandmother and an African Caribbean father. Several groups included parents of children of mixed heritage.

Eight of the groups met only once; one met twice; one met weekly for four months; one met weekly for eighteen months (excluding school holidays).

Sixty seven parents attended these group discussions: sixty women and seven men. Fifty nine women were white; one was Asian. Of the fifty nine white women, eight were known to have children of mixed heritage. Six men were white and one was African Caribbean. He had a child of mixed heritage.

In addition to these groups, the development worker was involved in initiating and running seventeen 'Drop In' groups with the Family Project worker. People who attended were offered the opportunity to participate in choosing how the 'Drop In' should be run as well as what sessions would be offered. People attending used the session as a way to gain general advice and have discussions about issues that affected their and their children's lives. Attendance at the sessions varied from eight to twenty people.

Some of the parents who gave their views in these groups were also involved in the project Steering Group, which was a source of further detailed information. The Steering Group had on it local parents, people from local voluntary workers groups, from health, education and community education, social services, NSPCC, the University and the local authority Area Management Team. This group met on seventeen occasions. Ten of the meetings were Steering Groups for local representatives only; a further seven included agency managers.

Seven women and one man asked to give their views individually to the development worker. Three of these met with the worker once; five met twice. These parents included three African Caribbean women, three white women and one white man and one woman whose ethnic origins were not known. Although the project was focusing on the views of parents, one African Caribbean child asked to give her views. Of the parents who spoke to the development worker individually, one had a child who had been sexually abused and was in care; one had had a very premature child and one had a child with a hearing impairment.

A social work student on placement with the Henley Safe Children Project was able to initiate and develop a small piece of work with parents with children who are disabled and parents themselves who are disabled. Because services and groups for the disabled were city wide rather than local and the student's time limited, it was decided to open up the geographical boundaries for this piece of work and encompass the whole city. Through this work the views of two groups of parents with children who are disabled were documented: thirty parents. One group was of white women, the other was of Asian parents with two men and thirteen women. The latter group included a parent who was himself disabled. In addition, individual interviews were carried out with three white parents who are disabled, one male and two female, as well as two white mothers who have a child who is disabled — in total thirty five parents' views were documented through this work.

Attempts were made by the Steering Group to find resources to work in schools, to provide children and young people with the opportunity to give their views on living in the area, and some of the difficulties they experienced. This suggestion came from parents on the Steering Group who felt that we should be recording children's views and feelings as well as parents'. They were keen to find out if children's views about living in the area were similar to or different from adults. The development worker did not have the time and opportunity to do this work. It remains an important area for further study and discussion to which a number of groups in the area continued to give attention.

The development worker was also involved with workers from other local agencies in designing, conducting and analysing two child care surveys in the area: already referred to in chapter one. Between them they covered the views of 197 parents — 131 white parents, 66 Black parents. The first survey funded by the Area Management Team was set up as part of a consultation to inform groups planning services under the 1989, Children Act. The survey was carried out to ensure that parents' and users views were included in this review of services, as concerns had been expressed that their views were underrepresented in the consultation process. When this survey was unsuccessful in discovering the views and experience of Black parents, the local authority Area Management Team provided resources to conduct a second survey, carried out by Black workers and workers experienced in working with Black communities, following consultation with Black groups city wide.

There were thirteen key workers from a wide range of statutory and voluntary health, welfare, and educational agencies who were involved extensively throughout the life of the project, as well as a group of local mothers, in providing continuous experience of local needs. They were also involved in the extensive liaison, networking, planning and development work which the Project engaged in. This work included:

- regular exchange of information;
- arranging access to premises, resources, funding;
- carrying out local surveys;
- organising presentations and training;
- devising family and children's support strategies;
- raising awareness of problems and issues;
- initiating and running groups.

Involvement in and discussions of all this work provided detailed material for the Henley Project. These key workers came from:

- Save the Children Fund;
- Wood End Family Project;
- Social Services Department;
- Local Authority Area Management Team;
- University of Warwick;
- Health Authority;
- OSABA — Educational, Cultural and Social Centre for African Caribbean Women and Children;
- Community Mediation Project.

The Director of the Home Office Safer Cities Project provided continuing support and back up, and advice about relevant activities and contacts.

The views of other workers from these agencies — as individuals and in groups — about the needs of families and children, were also documented. These have been summarised in Chapter 4.

There were many other agencies who provided valuable support and information; who followed up ideas and suggestions; who raised issues discussed during the course of the project amongst other groups and agencies within and outside Coventry. Some of their involvement will be referred to again in Chapter 6, along with some of the outcomes of work initiated by key workers during the course of the project. Whilst the contribution of the Henley Project's work in this wider arena cannot be measured, workers across the city and across the region have given very positive feedback about the influence of the project's explicit commitment to partnership and community development models, and its emphasis on the need for greater emphasis on preventive strategies and promoting wellbeing.

The induction phase of the project

During the first 4 months of the project the development worker made forty visits to agencies and individuals — most of them in the area which was the focus of the work — to introduce the aims of the project and build up a picture of the area. She gathered a great deal of information about local residents and services, how residents and workers viewed the area and how they thought it was perceived by people outside. All this was seen as essential preparation before making contact with parents to document their views. At the same time the University researcher began to gather material for an area profile.

It was during this period that the development worker started her attempts to make contact with organisations focusing on the needs of Black users of services across the city, to acknowledge the limitations of being a white worker in an area where it appeared that many agencies had little contact with Black groups. At the same time the NSPCC and University representatives were applying for funding to set up a parallel project to consult with Asian groups — who form a substantial minority in Coventry — about child protection and family support. The development worker was able to get agreement from local agencies that priority would be given to exploring how Black parents' views could be more fully represented in future work on children's and families' needs.

The Henley ward had been chosen as the project area because of its high child protection referrals. It was known that within the ward there were clusters of high referrals and of severe disadvantage. Mapping of referrals and information gathering about the characteristics of the area continued throughout the project. The development worker focused her attention on the districts with the highest referrals for child protection.

Local groups in or near those districts with an interest in child care and family support, health, education and social work teams in the area were visited, to explain the project and to gain their support. Joint work — according to group and agency priorities as well as those of the project — were discussed. Information about the districts, their residents, resources, strengths, activities and problems was gathered.

This provided invaluable contacts and information for the work of the next four months — mainly concerned with identifying parents who might be interested in the work of the project, either to give their views or join a steering group. Pilot sessions were run with two residents' groups on the experience of bringing up children in the area. Establishing good working relationships with such groups and with other workers in child care and family work, arranging joint work with them, was seen as a means of gaining access to a wide range of parents' views as well as furthering the collaborative aims of the project

Recruiting parents for the work of the project

Before recruitment was started, detailed attention was given to finding suitable premises for meetings, with good resources for looking after children. Making effective child care arrangements in suitable accommodation for children and for meetings with their parents was seen as essential preparation, to create a flexible framework within which to talk to and listen to parents and to document their views. Recruitment of parents was attempted in the following ways:

- approaching already existing community groups;

- mailing the statutory and voluntary agencies in the area asking workers to put us in touch with interested parents;
- by using outreach methods in parts of the area with only a few established community groups, for example leafleting outside local shops, schools and nurseries;
- by contacting statutory and voluntary agencies, some citywide, that had contact with particular sectors of the community, for example:
  - OSABA — educational, cultural and social centre for African Caribbean women and children;
  - Social Services agencies and voluntary groups, particularly for parents of children with disabilities or special needs, as well as parents themselves with a disability or special needs;
  - an Outreach Project; a support group organised by Community Education, to meet the needs of people with children of mixed racial heritage;
  - Wood End Family Project — a community development project based in a new purpose built centre, to encourage a range of community initiatives.

An information leaflet was devised in consultation with local parents and a local adult literacy class. They gave advice about the content, language and layout of the leaflet.

The leaflets invited local people to group meetings and to make individual contacts with the worker. They were given to all the individuals and groups with whom we had contact, to give them back up information about the project.

In preparing this leaflet, the development worker worked closely with the Family Project worker and put together a list of local agencies and resources which was then available for other groups in the area to use.

Leaflets were distributed in the following ways:

294 were mailed out to agencies

240 were sent out to parents with school children

420 were handed out personally by the development worker and a community education worker outside shops, a school and a nursery.

Childcare arrangements

Throughout the life of the project arrangements for childcare demanded careful organisation and took up a high proportion of the worker's time. In order to ensure that a wide range of parents could attend a variety of meetings, the following key pieces of work had to be undertaken:

- getting to grips with the new Children Act standards for creches
- finding suitable premises near enough to their homes and their children's schools;

- identifying suitably qualified creche workers and people who could act as temporary child minders;
- devising appropriate registration forms and parents' information leaflets about creches;
- ensuring appropriate equipment and refreshments for the creche were available;
- attending to practicalities of timing, support in meeting children from school etc.

Suitable premises

We had to find accommodation with a suitable room for childcare support and a comfortable room for parents to meet in with some privacy. Suitable tea and coffee making facilities were needed and smoking/non smoking spaces for the group had to be established. The premises had to be near where parents lived. Premises identified as best suited to the project's needs were the Wood End Family Project, a local nursery annexe, and the Henley Green Community Centre.

Information gathering phase

Creating a flexible framework/structure for group meetings

Originally we intended to try and run groups of interested parents for at least six weeks. This was to ensure that parents had time to:
- be clear about what the project was and whether they wanted to be involved;
- to feel comfortable enough to talk to each other about their needs in relation to their children;
- to allow time for them to be given any further information they may have wanted;
- to provide a positive, enjoyable experience for them and their children and give them something back for taking part in the project.

However, not all those who made contact with us wanted this. One group wanted to keep meeting beyond six weeks whilst others met only a couple of times and some only came once. Some of these got what they 'wanted to say off their chest' and did not come back. Follow up contacts with them suggested they were satisfied with this.

Information sharing

All participants were given clear information about the aims of the project, who was funding and managing it, what would happen to any information produced by individuals or groups. Concerns which they identified as important had to be followed up — such as finding out about activities, services and resources available to children; local child protection procedures — to ensure a reciprocal and respectful relationship between the worker and local people.

Confidentiality

Clear messages about confidentiality had to be given. The leaflet set out that:

> Confidentiality offered to parents will be based on a commitment to children's rights to protection and safety; this means that any information that suggests a child might have been harmed or be at serious risk will be passed on to the appropriate agency.

However, this principle had to be discussed in detail and understood by all individuals and groups.

Equal opportunities

Equal opportunities issues were given attention — a local Social Services nursery letter about creche rules and equal opportunities was used for creches, and ground rules were established by all groups about the language and behaviour which would be acceptable.

Running groups

The next seven months were mainly concerned with setting up and running groups. The development worker followed a similar pattern, whether working with individuals or groups. Whilst using the same basic framework, different groups worked very differently within this structure. Attempts were made to put everyone at ease through warm up exercises, and ensuring that everyone who wanted to contribute could do so, without feeling put on the spot. The aims of the project were stressed:
- to document parents' views about:
  - successes and difficulties in bringing up children
  - ways parents could help and support each other
  - how local services might best meet parents' needs and those of their children
- to encourage family support and self help initiatives which would promote the wellbeing of children.

The two figures which follow give examples of a typical group programme and a set of ground rules.

Table 8 Henley Safe Children Project: Programme for group discussion

Introduction — Warm up exercise, often in pairs.

A brief introduction to the Henley Safe Children Project, including issues around documenting parents' views, how this would be done and how confidentiality about who said what, could be kept.

The group set their own ground rules, but it was made clear that confidentiality offered to parents would be based on a commitment to children's rights to protection and safety. This meant that any information which suggested a child might have been harmed or be at serious risk would be passed on to the appropriate agency.

Sessions started with *looking at some good things about living in Wood End, Bell Green or Henley Green*, particularly linked to being a parent with children.

The services and groups they knew about in the areas they lived in were then listed.

We then moved on to looking at *the difficulties that parents had had* when bringing up children in Wood End, Bell Green and Henley Green.

Parents were asked to look at *what, if they had a magic wand* and could choose one thing, they thought would help support them in bringing up their children, living where they did. The importance of thinking about what they really wanted and needed was stressed.

We finished off with identifying one good and one bad thing about the session.

The following list of ground rules agreed by one group is fairly typical of those agreed in groups.

Table 9 Groundrules — Group A1

Confidentiality

Respect people's opinions

Smoke breaks at appropriate times.

Respect for visitors

No talking across others

Permission to disagree

Don't personalise disagreement

Don't ignore people

Be quiet if you want to

Apologise if possible in advance if you can't attend

Ensuring full local participation

The project had been set up following substantial discussions with voluntary and statutory agencies. A local multiagency steering group which would involve parents was seen as essential to the aims. Representatives could be nominated at the start of the project by local agencies, but substantial time was needed to involve local parents appropriately. The worker spent 6 months in discussion and consultation with local residents, groups and workers before it was felt that a sufficiently representative steering group could be formed.

The importance of waiting to hold the first steering group meeting until there was appropriate representation from local parents and carers was emphasised by one parent during a meeting held with the Family Support Group to evaluate the work of the local Area Management Team. When comparing being involved in the Henley Safe Children Project with the Family Support Group (both groups involved parents and local workers) she said that she 'had felt involved right from the start with the Henley group and part of it', whereas she felt 'lost, and didn't know what was going on' in the later group. In one group she felt ownership of the work, whereas in the other she felt she had been added on, to work others had defined and planned.

There was a substantial continuing involvement and participation by local parents. The group expanded gradually; it took a long time to gain involvement of people from the Henley Green area of the Project.

One particular group, associated with an Outreach initiative of the Community Education Department, did a great deal of work throughout the Henley Project. A number of them were on the Steering Group. The Steering Group had two strands:

a local group who met monthly:
- 6 parents
- Health Visitor
- Community Education Worker
- Headteacher
- Social worker from Local Social Services Department Team
- Development Worker — Henley
- Researcher/manager — Henley: chairperson

a wider group who attended three monthly meetings with the local group, mainly people with management responsibilities for services:
- Area Management Team
- Operational Services Manager — Social Services
- Safer Cities
- Community Safety Officer
- School Governor
- Health Manager

To ensure that the Steering Group meetings worked effectively, attention was given to:

- clarifying the roles and functions of the group and its different members;
- providing a local, comfortable venue — the newly opened Family Project — for the meetings; taking into account and overcoming barriers to access to the meeting that local parents/residents might experience, for example providing childcare support if needed, usually a creche; running meetings within school hours — to allow parents to drop off children and pick them up from school;
- providing an informal structure for the meetings, with tea, coffee and biscuits at the beginning and middle of the meetings to encourage people to feel relaxed and comfortable;
- starting meetings with introductions to ensure everyone knew everyone and their roles;
- the chairperson ensuring that everyone had a chance to speak;
- arranging for the minutes to be taken by someone not involved in the meeting;
- paying transport expenses if parents needed them;
- using Key Points about Participation as a checklist when organising all meetings (See Appendix I).

Relationships with other workers

The aim of the project to work collaboratively with local workers and encourage discussions of developments which were needed, demanded careful liaison with other workers, and was essential to establishing and maintaining good contacts with a range of parents in different circumstances. The development worker worked closely with others in the voluntary and statutory sectors to consider in detail what the views and experiences of parents meant for services in the area; to listen to their views about priorities for parents and children; to identify and find ways of filling gaps in local service provision and to ensure ready access to supportive services for parents who might raise personal difficulties.

Key local workers and managers were involved in the Henley Safe Children Project Steering Group. The development worker attended numerous local networks and forum meetings, for example:

locally	the Under 5s Managers Group
	the Wood End/Bell Green Area Children Act Early Years Forum
	the Family Support Group — co-ordinated by the Area Management Team after the Henley Project began
citywide	as a voluntary sector representative on the Central Coordinating Panel of the Children Act Review of Services for children under 8
	the Women's Development Network
	the Coventry Community Childcare Network

The development worker became involved in the Coventry Community Childcare Network as a result of her concerns about the lack of support available for anyone who was running childcare provision, particularly creches. The implementation of the Children Act 1989 and the local management of schools were all affecting the provision of creches and some facilities were lost during the period of the project.

The worker had originally, alongside other workers in the voluntary sector, tried to address some of these issues locally. This was in response to local parents making it clear that they felt there were not enough childcare facilities in the area to meet their needs. However after several attempts to set up and sustain groups through WHEB (Wood End, Henley Green and Bell Green) and the Creche Development Network citywide, it was agreed to join forces with the Coventry Community Childcare Network, which mainly dealt with nursery provision in the non profit making sector.

Although WHEB and The Creche Development Network did not meet regularly, they still provided workers with an opportunity to keep each other informed about the implementation of the Children Act 1989, the Under 8s Review and the Regulation of Childcare for Under 8s, as well as the progress of each other's work. The development worker was therefore able to write and raise concerns of group members about the way the Under 8s Review was carried out. The worker raised with the Core Group (Under 8s Review Consultation) several points on behalf of other voluntary sector groups, including the following:

> Whilst accepting that you feel that opportunities to involve users of day care facilities for Under 8s have been provided, our group would be very interested to know the numbers of parents who have attended the consultancy or at least the proportion of parents' views to professional views recorded.

> We would like to re-assert our concern outlined in our last letter, namely:

> 'The group's main concern is that 'users' views and experiences are not being adequately addressed by the review process. The voluntary sector have a great deal of expertise and experience of working with 'users' in partnership. Although some specific sectors of the voluntary sector have been targeted for their expertise and views (and this has been resourced) we believe that a great deal of expertise, is being neglected, not valued and overlooked and therefore not resourced.'

> ... particularly with reference to the next review which I understand is to take place by October 1995. We would hope that practical barriers to parents attending forums will be addressed in consultation with local voluntary sector organisations.

Although we feel that it has been positive to have had forums to ensure that Black parents and parents with children with disabilities were heard, we are worried that:

• Linkages between forums have been lost or missed. It is not clear that some views have been made across the board not just by a few unhappy parents.

• Views that are minority views appear to have been marginalised and therefore Action Plans do not lead to any resources being allocated to these issues.

The response to these points was:

It is acknowledged that the first phase of the review did not facilitate enough the expression of parents' or users' views. Greater efforts to achieve this were made in the second part of the review, but it would still be accurate to say that more professionals than parents were involved, although the views expressed by each group were not always different. I recognise that in respect of each action point, the involvement of 'users' will need to be addressed; it might be useful for us to meet at some stage to discuss this.

There has been no intention to 'marginalise' the views of any minority group and care was taken to highlight views expressed in a number of forums across the city. There is a general, severe resource problem, and, as you may know from the local press, cuts in Under 5s provision are anticipated. However, the review places us in a good position to argue for re-direction of resources to meet new requirements and much of the action points can be achieved within existing resources.

The development worker tried to ensure that issues raised about children's needs in any of the groups she worked with were continuously fed back into the project's work and communicated with relevant local agencies.

Regular meetings and contacts were maintained with numerous local workers, for example:
• Community Education Outreach workers
• Community Development Worker for Wood End Family Project and Save the Children Fund
• Community Safety Officer
• OSABA Childcare Development Worker
• Community Education/Adult Literacy Worker in Henley Green

Attention was paid throughout the project to ensuring two way exchanges of information and discussions of issues between parents and workers related to local service provision. This was achieved through:
• the Steering Group, which had monthly meetings, involving local workers, project staff and parents, and three monthly meetings which involved local authority and health service managers.

- ensuring that parents involved in the Henley Safe Children Project were invited to a wide range of appropriate meetings e.g. Family Support Group, a sub group of the local authority district management team or Area Management Team; a local interagency Domestic Violence Forum.
- encouraging and supporting parents in communicating their ideas about services, either in person or in writing, to service providers; facilitating their involvement with other groups developing services or gathering information e.g. in childcare surveys; writing to the Health Authorities about child and parent friendly facilities at hospitals and doctors' surgeries and to local authority departments e.g. Community Parks Consultation.

As the project was time limited and did not have the resources to provide any new services, the emphasis throughout was on bringing together those who might be able to shape future services.

The dissemination phase of the project

The final stage of the Project was the dissemination phase. The main phase of the dissemination took place from April 1993 to July 1993 as planned. However presentations and consultations on the work of the Henley Safe Children Project had actually started in November 1992 and continued throughout 1995. They continued after that through the work of the New Links Project.

This dissemination phase was seen as the key time for ensuring that parents' views were passed on to agencies and workers. However it was not the only time that this occurred. Parent's views were being passed on to agencies during the whole of the project through the Steering Group and the various networking groups mentioned earlier.

Preparation for presentations

All parents whose views had been documented through the project were offered the opportunity to give their views to agencies and workers in whatever manner they wished. Most parents chose to have their views, concerns and experiences written down by the development worker and then gave permission for the project to pass these on to agencies. Parents from Group A prepared a basic leaflet themselves that outlined their and their children's key needs and also spent a great deal of time preparing a formal presentation of their and other parent's views. None of the parents involved in preparing for and making presentations had done this before.

After much discussion and debate the parents felt that the presentation should consist of:

A background to the work of Henley Safe Children Project and a breakdown of relevant statistics on the area:

- the development worker, Lyn Carruthers
- sometimes the manager/researcher Norma Baldwin.

A message from parents living in the area on trying to bring up healthy, happy and safe children, based on their experiences
- all parents.

A brief summary of all parents' views, concerns and issues as documented for the Henley Safe Children Project
- the development worker.

Finally an overview of the key aspects of a preventive strategy based on the findings of the Henley Safe Children Project
- the development worker and/or researcher.

Thirteen slides and thirteen overheads were used to support the parents' part of the presentation: all devised and prepared by the parents. This would take approximately twenty minutes, the floor would then be opened for questions, comments and discussion on the issues raised. An information pack was given to participants, on the work of the Henley Safe Children Project.

In the later stages of the dissemination, information was also given about parents' views and experiences of the participative style of the project and contrasting experience of previous consultations.

Groups and agencies invited to disseminations were offered a one hour or two hour slot, and chose according to their commitments.

Originally it had been planned to offer presentations to agencies individually. Although some agencies took this offer up, for example the police and a housing association, most preferred to pick a date out of several on offer and attend with a mixed group. A few presentations were made to one, two or three people only. Parents and the development worker agreed to this as they wanted to ensure as many people as possible heard the findings of the project, and they were aware of how busy people were. Having this flexibility allowed more people to attend over all. Most presentations were given to groups of 10 to 20. A few had more than 75.

The presentations were made during school hours (between 9.15 am – 3.00 pm) to be convenient to parents. Childcare was provided for parents or participants if needed, as well as transport or reimbursement of travelling expenses. Where the bulk of participants were local to the area, local venues were used.

Substantial time was given for preparation, over several months. Parents involved preferred to integrate their involvement in the project with the rest of their lives and family commitments, so work needed to be done in two hour sessions spread out over several months.

There had to be enough time for taking photographs, writing, devising overheads, learning to use screens, overhead and slide projectors. Without this extensive preparation and the debates and discussions about it, parents would not have felt ready to face agencies and organisations with their views.

Careful planning was needed to ensure that parents could take part in the public presentations. It was agreed that we would offer an absolute maximum of three sessions in any one week, and general group disseminations would be planned over a four to five week period. This worked well and allowed parents to take part without having to put too much of their life on hold.

Arrangements for presentations

There are two examples below of the arrangements that were made to ensure successful presentation sessions.

In one of the early presentations, a workshop run for local workers on the findings of the Henley Safe Children Project, with an additional aim to find out workers' views on parents' and children's needs in the area, three mothers chose to be involved. We already had our presentation worked out, but we still needed to meet to discuss how we would run the workshop and record the meeting. The session ran from 2.00 pm – 4.00 pm. Three different types of childcare provision were used:

    1) one child was looked after by her father at home
    2) a creche was provided from 2.00 – 3.00 pm
    3) a session with play workers was used from 3.00 – 4.00 pm.

As the session ran on past school hours we arranged a break in the session for tea and coffee and the speakers went off to collect their children from school. We managed to collect the children from school, give them juice and biscuits and introduce them to the playworkers, all within 15 minutes (the schools were nearby). Transport was provided for one parent who lived further away.

The workshop and presentation were structured to allow for flexibility, using short presentations, question and answer sessions, informal summarising, writing up on flip charts to make everyone feel comfortable and be encouraged to take part. It went very well: there was a friendly constructive atmosphere and a great deal of information was collected from the workers.

In the second example, NCH Action for Children invited us to make a presentation to their regional managers and workers. They get 10 out of 10 for their support!

    • They moved their regional meeting to Coventry to make it more convenient for us.
    • The National Children's Homes project at which the meeting was held provided us all, including children, with lunch (it was during the school holidays).
    • The Project provided childcare for the children who attended — they had a great time, the lunch was great too.
    • They helped us set up and were very encouraging.

• Participants valued what was said.
• They paid all our expenses, provided lunch and childcare and paid us as speakers as well.

The first open, public presentation of the project's work took place in November 1992 at the NSPCC's Regional Seminar 'Is Preventing Child Abuse a Reality in the 1990s?' held in Leamington Spa. Preparation for this presentation involved the whole of parents' group A, although Norma Baldwin, Lyn Carruthers and two parents actually made the formal presentation. Two other parents, who had wanted to attend but not speak, stood by a Henley Safe Children Project stall over the lunch break and were inundated with questions and requests for leaflets from people attending the Seminar. This presentation was very well received and all the parents were complimented for their contributions by people attending. Professionals provided feedback over a lengthy period saying that what the parents had said had really stayed with them and had had a powerful impact on them.

The second major public presentation was made at the Fourth European Conference on Child Abuse and Neglect held in Padua, Italy at the end of March 1993. Getting to and giving a presentation at this Conference was made possible by support from the Applied Social Studies Department at Warwick University and a charitable trust. They paid for the development worker and two parents to attend the conference, as well as the researcher. Again the whole of parents' group A prepared for this presentation, this time with very little notice. The group took photographs, prepared and chose slides and made up overheads for the presentation as well as agreeing on the key messages that they wanted the two parents attending to convey. This presentation was well received by more than 50 professionals from around the world. It was one of the only presentations that received a spontaneous round of applause! The two mothers were listed as authors in the Book of the Papers presented to the Conference. They felt that they had a rewarding — if unnerving — experience. Attending this Conference was seen by them and others involved as recognition of their hard work and creative efforts.

As might be expected, the process by which the two parents were chosen to attend the Conference was fraught with difficulties. One parent felt that she had not been given a proper opportunity to choose whether she should go or not. As a result of her dissatisfaction she then left the group. However, all the other group members supported the way the decision was taken — with the financial sponsors offering the money for the group who had already given a successful public presentation. The rest of the group were accepting of this arrangement, seeing it as a group presentation. Although the parent who left the group did not return to the group she still kept an interest in the work of the project and discussed progress with the development worker.

In this early period of dissemination, other presentations were given to the Coventry Area Child Protection Committee, to the University of Warwick's course in Child Protection and its Diploma in Social Work.

These early presentations over a period of six months, of their views and concerns, gave the group of mothers involved a chance to try out and correct their contributions. They had found it hard to believe that anyone would want to hear them talking about their views and said they 'really only had a go initially to see how it went'. After the response to the first presentation in Leamington, the mothers could see that not only did people listen to them, but that professionals thought their part was the most valuable and memorable part of the conference. They were told this by professionals on the day. Parents comments were 'It was good — we felt really good. It did a lot for our confidence'.

After the International Conference in Italy parents said:

It was brilliant. It was challenging. Never felt so good after we'd done it. I was nervous but I felt really good. Felt confident — had all the confidence in the world afterwards. Proud of ourselves. I didn't think there would be so many people as there was. Didn't think anyone would want to listen to us.

We felt people listened to us more because we were parents. We created more of an impact because we were parents.

This positive response from professionals helped to encourage parents to see the value of offering their presentation to agencies involved in child protection work.

The group of mothers reduced from seven down to four during this period, as some felt that they did not want to be involved in giving formal presentations. This was entirely their choice. They did maintain contact however. Only four mothers chose to be involved in the intensive dissemination phase. Each chose how much involvement she wanted to have. One parent preferred to put on the overheads and answer questions and queries at the end rather than speak during the presentation. The group agreed this was fine. However by the end of this phase all of them were taking turns at making presentations.

The four mothers split up into two pairs. Whilst one pair spoke the other pair operated the slide projector and put on the overheads. The pairs then alternated between presentations. This made the presentations slightly different as each mother wrote her own part, but the themes and concerns were the same.

Payment for presentations

From the initial part of the dissemination phase it had been planned to recognise and value parents efforts as speakers by paying them as trainers. Several applications for funding were made to ensure that this was possible. Applications were not always successful. A small sum of money was eventually identified from Safer Cities and University funding so that parents could be paid a contribution towards all their hard work. Payments were made which did not affect their entitlement to benefits.

Two parents continued to make presentations and run workshops on the work of the Henley Safe Children Project and their views on partnerships in child protection work after the project ended. They were invited to make presentations at Conferences and training events.

Dissemination to local agencies

Between April and June 1993 the development worker spent most of her time writing to, following up and arranging presentations for statutory and voluntary agencies, locally and citywide. The list of agencies and individuals to be invited had been drawn up by the Henley Safe Children Project Steering Group. During this phase of the project, although everyone received a written invitation, most of the work was done on the phone. The development worker rang before letters arrived to let people know to expect an invitation and then called again when agencies had had time to deal with it. Doing this ensured that the invitations received priority and that agencies and individuals were clear about the unique opportunity that was being offered. There was clearly a much better response to the phone calls than the letter, which would have been likely to become buried under a pile of other paperwork judging from initial calls made by the development worker.

It became clear that the good response to the invitations was due to the initial leg work done by the development worker during her intensive induction period. People had at least heard about the project, even if they didn't know much about it. This was also a very appropriate time to be offering agencies users' views of their services, and information about needs for child care and protection and family support.

Agencies were very keen to hear from parents themselves about their experiences of bringing up children in Wood End, Henley Green and Bell Green. Their keenness is reflected in the list of representatives attending dissemination sessions:

The Local Authority: Health Agencies
   Chief Executive's Dept   The Home Office
   Community Education   Politicians
   Economic Development   Voluntary Sector
   Education   West Midlands Police Force
   Environmental Services   West Midlands Probation Service
   Housing
   Leisure
   Social Services

Altogether 23 presentations and consultations were made by the development worker and parents during the period November '92 — July '94. Three hundred and twenty-seven people attended these presentations. The vast majority were professionals involved in child protection or children's health and welfare. This does not include sessions individuals have had with the development worker, to discuss the work of the Henley Safe Children Project, how it was set up, its findings and recommendations, which have been numerous.

The NSPCC itself was keen to hear what parents from the project were saying. A national policy development officer attended one of the dissemination sessions. The Director of the NSPCC and the National Director of Children's Services also visited the project to hear about the findings and to meet the parents involved. A presentation of the findings of the project was made by the development worker and a parent at the Benjamin Waugh Foundation's Annual Forum in London, at the Policy Studies Institute. (The Benjamin Waugh Foundation consists of supporters who give a minimum of £500 per year or more to NSPCC Funds).

As part of the dissemination process the development worker worked with a journalist on an article for the Coventry Evening Telegraph on the findings of the project. This article appeared in June 1993.

The Audit Commission took evidence from the project, as part of its work for the report 'Seen but not heard' (1994).

Once the bulk of the dissemination sessions were completed, by summer 1993, the development worker and the mothers evaluated the sessions, their involvement in them and the work of the Henley Safe Children Project overall.

The following are some of the comments of mothers about their involvement in the presentations:

> Gave us a chance to talk about things that we believe in and that are very important, to the right people, not just to each other.

> Has given us credibility.

> The community have benefited and will benefit from the skills, confidence, expertise, experience and information gathered that we have built up during the Henley Safe Children Project.

> We've all grown from it, not frightened to speak our minds, our views therefore other projects we are involved in will benefit from this not just ourselves.

> Things can change. We can influence things — it is possible — although maybe slowly.

> It has made agencies aware of parents' expectations.

> Now we're not frightened to say what we think and want.

18 months ago I would have moaned about things in my own home, now I would stand up and say things in public.

The presentation at Leamington did this; didn't really understand the impact this would have on ourselves, the group and the project — gave us more confidence to speak to people we didn't know.

After Leamington, realised that people would listen. After Leamington, felt like a team and all in it together.

The dissemination sessions were organised, so we'll do them. Did not know what they'd achieve. Trusted Lyn and believed we should do it.

Now we think it is important and would encourage people to make presentations, to talk to people who need to know.

I could do it anywhere, anytime, any place now.

Parents also mentioned how they felt the presentations affected the people who attended them. They stated:

Some of the workers were shocked at some of the background statistics at Wood End, Bell Green and Henley Green, for example, number of children on the Child Protection Register in the area. The interagency discussions were good and informative. People seemed to enjoy the opportunity to talk to each other about the issues raised.

The health visitors were shocked at the statistics and some of the things that happened in the area. They thought it was a good project and it is important that parents' voices get heard.

I think it meant more to them to hear from first hand experiences of parents about the difficulties of trying against all odds to bring up their children, so they can be happy, healthy and safe.

I think we all went away feeling that we had all learnt something.

Professionals frequently used the parents at the presentations as consultants on issues or plans relevant to their services or work. As one parent pointed out:

After the presentation, instead of talking about the project and what we wanted, we ended up being interviewed about issues of concern to some of the people present.

The development worker and parents also did an evaluation of the venues that were used during the presentations. The venues that were most user friendly were the ones that:

made us all feel welcome (children included);

had facilities for all of us (children included);

had friendly staff who made sure that we felt welcomed;

where we were able to concentrate on our presentations rather than sorting out difficulties with the premises.

It had been difficult for the development worker to find even five venues which technically met the requirements. The requirement least likely to be met was a room suitable for providing childcare.

Of the premises used, only three out of five were considered suitable in practice. All the suitable ones were in the voluntary rather than statutory sector.

The four parents who were involved throughout the dissemination phase of the project said they enjoyed themselves and felt it really built up their confidence. They had opportunities to build up credit from their work under the NVQ scheme.

Experiences of local people when engaging with agencies and professionals.

By the end of the Henley Safe Children Project, parents involved in the Steering Group and the dissemination and consultation sessions had had extensive experience of working with a wide range of workers — from local grass roots workers, to managers of organisations and services. All through the project the development worker and parents had discussed their feelings about being involved in the work of the project, and their views about workers' responses to them as parents. When asked about their involvement generally in the project, parents commented:

For once had a group that's done something.

Its the first thing I've taken seriously — have turned up, made it a priority.

It came at the right time.

We were praised for our presentation skills.

There was a good worker who encouraged us.

When further questioned about what they meant by a good worker the group said that it was the worker's attitude they were talking about:

That she wouldn't tell us the answers.

She made us work.

She didn't prompt us into making decisions — it was all our own thoughts.

You feel as if you've made the decision yourself.

You are doing it because you want to.

Other comments from the group continued:

> I've had a long term commitment — been working on the same topic for 18 months, haven't done this before, been involved in short courses. Felt strongly about the topic 'close to my heart'. As the project had an end target I felt I could commit myself to 18 months.

> There's an end result to it. Done lots of courses which were tasters. In one way it was good as knew it had to be done by October therefore there was a target — had to get on with it. It had clear aims, targets and time schedules. I know what was expected of me.

> You need to have a light at the end of the tunnel.

> It's important to have created a document that can be used in the future for reference, because it's got parents' views in it. These can be compared with future reports. It's got real life situations in it.

> It's how we felt — it's written down.

> As a parent it's made you feel that you've achieved something as a parent. It highlights parents' skills and objectives not just parenting skills, but other skills and concerns. It's like having a job you have to plan, write, speak etc.

> I don't think parents get the credit they are due, and they don't expect to be credited for example, 'I'm only a housewife or mother' as if it's nothing.

> Parents are getting the blame for society and the community breakdown as individual units but parenting skills are not valued and parents are not supported or encouraged for doing a good job. Children's futures are everybody's responsibility.

After having these more general discussions about being involved in the project, parents then moved on to talk more specifically about what partnership with professionals meant for them.

Parents had positive and negative experiences when talking to professionals, especially during the dissemination phase of the project. Negative experiences led parents to state:

> It was really hard work to get them to participate. They were expecting to be talked at, not discuss issues.

> We felt like we had been put in a glass bowl. They didn't participate, talk or ask questions. It felt like they were talking to Norma and Lyn, not to us. This made us feel belittled.

> I felt the officers were only there because they were told they had to be there. (I know because they told us this at the door.) They were very patronising,

> they spoke mostly to Lyn. I felt like they were listening to Lyn and not to us because they are professionals.

However, positive experiences in sessions prompted the following comments:

> Learnt from them about their work for example, a guardian ad litem. Lots of questions and there was a good discussion. They talked to us not just Norma and Lyn.

> People were really interested and we think they will take ideas back from this — about involving parents and local people. We were praised for our presentation skills and for going and speaking to them.

> This was a really nice afternoon, the atmosphere and acceptance of a group of mums felt warm and welcoming. I think they and our group could have talked all day and still not have become bored.

Parents were very astute in their assessments and even when they received a positive response initially were quick to recognise when they were being dismissed or patronised.

> They were all in agreement with us, they didn't disagree. However, they did say it's a terrible situation to be in but, well what can we do — it's like this everywhere.

> We ended up feeling defensive and like 'whining women', and that we were moaning about things. We didn't achieve very much at this meeting.

> There was quite a lot of interest shown and our group was congratulated about the way we put our point across, but not many felt inclined to ask questions about the project but seemed to have to say how unexpected and professional our presentation was.

> We did our presentation then he did his on how good his service was in the area and the improvements they'd made recently. He said that we were different to other residents in Wood End, Bell Green and Henley Green.

> I think these people had their own views about families in Wood End and Henley Green well before they came to our presentation and weren't really prepared to alter their opinions even after they had seen and heard what we had to say.

Parents also complained about being asked to conferences and seminars that ran on past school hours, which meant having to miss important parts of the day:

> We had to leave before the end to get home for children so missed speakers and plenary.

It wasn't lack of funds which meant parents couldn't stay, it was the complex nature of making suitable childcare arrangements for their older school children which made it much simpler and more satisfactory to return home in time. Only for very special or exceptional occasions were arrangements successfully made, which involved partners taking leave from work or taking over responsibility for childcare, or grandparents helping out with childcare. This did not always run smoothly.

This material was later used as the basis for a presentation entitled 'Parents, Participation and Prevention, Your Expectations, What About Ours?', in part of a Study Day for Birmingham Child Protection Committee, looking at Prevention Strategies, in June 1994. It has also been presented to a workshop held at Bristol University, in July 1994, for the BASPCAN Second National Congress on the theme 'Working in Partnership'.

Why parents got involved in talking to agencies

Parents involved in the dissemination sessions became involved in the Henley Safe Children Project to get child protection professionals to listen to what it is like trying to bring up children safely in the area. One parent said:

> I think even before I got involved in the Project I wasn't happy about things that were going on around me, that I was having to live amongst.

> I'm not blinkered and some of what I saw and heard about, I didn't like just to ignore, shrug my shoulders and hope it went away the day after tomorrow. Even feeling that way, I didn't know what I could do to try to change things.

> I was warned, after only 24 hours of moving into the area, to turn and look the other way if I saw anyone trying to break into someone else's house. That comment was noted but not taken notice of.

Parents saw what happened to children everyday around them. They didn't want just to leave it, they wanted to do something about it, but they didn't know *what* to do, *who* to talk to about their concerns. They were living with a very real fear of intimidation and reprisals if they tried to do something.

> Everyday we see what happens to children on the street and we aren't happy with this. Because we care we wanted to talk about our concerns and try to change things for the better.

> We wanted to be able to tell people that we don't normally get a chance to reach, how parents feel about the pressures of living on this estate. We also felt that as residents of this estate we are often treated as second class citizens by policy makers therefore our views as parents are not valued. Taking part in

the Henley Safe Children Project gave us an opportunity to have our views valued.

It's been important to meet with social workers, health visitors and other workers involved in child protection work to talk to them about their work and our experiences. We aren't their clients and this means that we can talk more easily about how it really feels living here.

Parents also wanted to find out about child protection issues, agencies' roles and responsibilities. They had often heard about people's negative experiences — they wanted to know what it's really about — how to protect children from harm? They wanted to have the opportunity to do something. Parents learned a lot from being involved in the Project.

Being involved in this project helped us recognise and value the skills that we already had. We have been encouraged to use these skills to achieve things that previously ourselves and other people would have thought impossible. Our self confidence and self esteem have improved. We now feel able to disagree with people openly, we can make ourselves vulnerable to criticism and we have something to say and are listened to when we say it.

Parents involved have begun to challenge other parents about their views of child protection services.

The stigma is so bad for social services and NSPCC in this area, that even if you're involved in positive things it is often viewed by other residents initially as: what are you doing with *them*? what have *you* done — to your kids? People think you've done something because you are involved with them.

Whereas now as a result of positive participation and partnership with the NSPCC and social services people's views have changed. For example with relatives, my mum tells people at work what I do, my children tell their friends. Also at the school people think what I do is really good even though they don't know exactly what I do. They say I'd love to be able to do something like you do. They ask what help and support services are available for them and their children.

Fear of child protection services

Although not all parents mentioned fear of child protection services when their views were documented, most did discuss this initially with the development worker. This was mentioned by local workers, a number of whom had told the development workers that 'no-one will speak to you when they find out that you work for the N.S.P.C.C. and have links with social services'.

This was certainly a barrier that needed to be overcome. It was over-come in part by giving parents a chance to express their fears and discussing the child protection issues that came out of their concerns. These discussions were frequently heated and full of strong feelings. People had their feelings recognised and gained more information about child protection procedures. The development worker found that parents were more willing to give their views and have them documented even in uncomfortable and fraught sessions if they had been given factual information about child protection systems and procedures.

Challenges of engaging with agencies and workers

Although, by and large, parents had positive experiences of engaging with professionals in discussions about child protection issues they also observed and were on the receiving end of behaviour that was unhelpful. The following list was devised, based on their actual experiences of pro-fessionals during the time of the project. This is their list of do's and don'ts if you want to encourage parents to be involved!

Table 10 Parents, partnership, participation and prevention: your expectations, what about ours?

- don't fall asleep
- don't make it obvious that you don't want to be there or that you've been ordered to come
- do make eye contact with us
- don't use defensive body language
- don't turn up after the session has finished
- don't patronise us
- let us make our own decisions, rather than tell us what to do
- don't praise yourself for being there
- don't use fancy titles to put us down
- do listen to what we've got to say
- be prepared to be challenged, learn to take positive criticism
- encourage us to participate
- don't come in to teach us, come in to learn and share
- don't label us and we won't label you
- don't tell us what can't be done, we'll tell you what can be done
- remember we aren't different to everybody else on the estate because we care
- we're grateful that you are listening to us, but you should be grateful that we are talking to you
- we don't have to be paid, but it would be nice sometimes

They then went on to talk about how these bad experiences of consulta-tion made them feel:

Table 11　Bad experiences of consultation will make us feel:

- more determined
- angry
- ignored
- defensive
- insecure
- suspicious - why are you here?
- more cautious
- hurt
- uncertain
- frustrated
- vulnerable
- that we don't exist
- not respected
- bored
- less confident
- more careful
- confused
- like the underdog

The effects of this behaviour were described as:
- we're there but not taking part
- we won't come again
- our current views of your organisation are reinforced, for example you aren't sensitive to our needs
- we are less likely to co-operate or participate in future events
- we will pass on our negative experiences to friends, relatives groups, meetings, training that we attend.

Parents then talked about how good experiences made them feel:

Table 12　Good experiences of consultation will make us feel:

- equal to others
- encourage us to keep going — to carry on
- it will make us feel more enthusiastic
- we will feel as if people have taken notice of what we said
- confident we can do it — we get a buzz
- we feel proud
- feel valued
- respected

This will result in:
- lots of positive participation
- we will take on more responsibilities and be willing to be involved in things
- our views of your organisation will become more realistic
- we will be committed to what we are involved in
- we will pass on positive experiences of being involved to friends, relatives, groups, meetings, training we attend.

Issues in community development work

Women only?

The development worker, managers, a vast majority of workers, local people and others associated with the project were women. Whilst issues of men's responsibility for and involvement in childcare were permanently on our agenda, we nevertheless in our structure and practice continued to reflect a common expectation that childcare and child protection work are women's responsibility. Our attention and very limited resources were focused on *parents'* views of what was needed in the area to ensure the safety and wellbeing of children, but it was very largely *mothers* who became and remained involved. This is a common experience in all childcare work, and very common in community development work more broadly. Efforts were made to raise consciousness of the need to involve men much more centrally in finding solutions to some of the problems of the area, in joint work with the Family Project, with the Community Safety Officer, Community Education, and the Area Management Team. These groups continue work on these issues.

We see it as a weakness of our project, however, that in practice our working methods could be seen to reinforce women's responsibilities in childcare, in an area where many single mothers already shoulder enormous burdens. The media coverage during the course of the project, of the views of government and other groups, about the threat posed to social order by single mothers, caused much debate. A consensus of opinion in the project was that these views were extreme and unrealistic. Many single mothers were in the forefront of a struggle to maintain standards of decency and a safe caring community. Their role in preventing further deterioration in disadvantaged neighbourhoods was crucial.

Many of the issues identified by parents related to problems with 'macho' behaviour and culture of young people. A commonly held view was that whilst males — in expectations and behaviour — presented major problems in the area, there were also a number of young women identified with a hostile and destructive culture. Proportions of offenders taken to court in the area were overwhelmingly higher amongst males. Some workers and parents associated with the project had particular concerns about the level of domestic violence and its implication for child protection. With hindsight, we would have preferred to challenge the 'women only' approach more substantially in our structure and working methods, had resources been available. The involvement of fathers in discussions of child care needs, roles of males in caring, would repay focused work in its own right.

Considerable success was achieved in improving participation by local residents and carers in consultations and decisions about service provision in the area. Ensuring that children's views and feelings are taken seriously still has a long way to go, although some gains are being made. Their views have been taken account of in planning the local park and two groups have been established where young people can meet to discuss issues that arise from being a teenager.

During the course of the project the Steering Group came to a view that school children's views of their experience in the area would provide essential complementary information to that of parents. There were not the resources needed for this additional work within the project, however efforts continued to find additional resources to do this through community education workers and local people.

Minority groups

Issues in involving Black and other minority ethnic groups and in involving children and parents with disabilities have been mentioned throughout. Resources appropriate to recognise and value differences and to ensure involvement were essential. Differences had to be acknowledged and respected, and timescales adjusted to do this. Targeting minority groups can have negative as well as positive consequences. By working separately, we can continue exclusion. Some of the contradictions involved in trying to engage in antioppressive and non discriminatory work from agencies where equal opportunities were far from being achieved were a source of continuing concern. Some of these issues continue to be worked on through the New Links Project, which built on the work of the Henley Project and continues as a neighbourhood support initiative and through the Asian Children and Families Project (Atkar et al. 1997), as well through all the agencies which supported the Henley Project.

We cannot claim that the parents we worked with provide a representative sample of groups in the Henley ward, nor that their experiences are typical. We did make substantial efforts, however, to engage with minority groups through a wide range of agencies, through networking and through extensive publicity.

Even so it is likely that some of the parents who are most isolated and vulnerable will not have been reached. This continues to be addressed particularly through the New Links Project.

Childcare

Some of the practical and emotional demands on parents who worked with the project have been described in earlier chapters. Caring for young children, often with very limited financial and social resources, was a continuing pressure on all those who worked with us in the project. For all parents, but particularly for mothers on their own, or who had partners who had had to go out of the area to find work, the day to day organisation of their households demanded high levels of skill and inventiveness. Giving time to attend interviews, meetings, consultations, to gathering or disseminating information about child protection and family support needs, working with professionals to plan and implement local strategies, called for a level of organisation of daily demands and unexpected crises which workers in structured, rationalised jobs may not always fully recognise. A very high proportion of the development worker's time was spent in providing or supporting child care arrangements such as creches, playworkers, child minders, sitting services, transport for mothers and children, to ensure that full participation was possible.

Taking full account of the day to day responsibilities of those caring for others is a time consuming and costly business. Caring work has generally been undervalued in comparison with other forms of work (Finch and Groves 1983; Graham 1983; Dalley, 1988). Taken for granted assumptions about its gendered and invisible nature may provide obstacles to the level of commitment and resourcing needed to make progress in community development work. Yet the benefits to be gained from improvements in local morale and wellbeing can be enormous. Major resources of skill, increasing time and commitment can be released, when pressures of caring lessen.

Practicalities of involvement

The breakdown of individual childcare arrangements — for example one child being too ill to go to school, or a parent needing an emergency medical consultation — could lead to cancellation of meetings, loss of momentum, frustration. Initiatives could fail because the meeting place had to be closed unexpectedly. For example one group were due to meet for a third time in a centre which was closed suddenly because of flea infestation. It had taken a great deal of work and persuasion to get these people to the first two meetings, in an area where there were very few existing groups. After the third meeting was cancelled due to the fleas, the group lost its momentum and did not meet again. It took 2 to 3 weeks to open the building again and that was too late. Because many of those who would have attended did not have telephones, communication had been by letter — which might have been a further influence on feelings of low involvement.

Some premises were unsuitable — for example some school halls had only children's chairs; some were used for school meals, leaving lingering smells; some offered no privacy.

Flexible childcare arrangements are very difficult to provide on an ad hoc basis. The same creche workers or child minders may not be available to provide continuity for relatively short periods, or sessions which may not have a long preparation time, or any regularity of demand. Some workers may already be at the limit of what they can earn without losing benefit. Qualified or experienced childcare workers providing a flexible part time service to get back into work, may use this as a stepping stone to more permanent jobs. Information about availability of experienced childcare workers may be hard to find: there was no city wide list, although there was a city wide private agency who could provide creche workers for short periods.

A range of personal reasons kept mothers from attending some planned meetings, including:
- appendix operation
- emergency admission to hospital, following collapse
- being offered a part time job
- clash of meetings with other voluntary groups
- partner getting leave from a job in another part of the country.

Not attending sessions did not necessarily mean a lack of interest or commitment. Follow up and support for individuals was often very important, as well as the group focused work.

Information about services and supports available, voluntary work and projects, was not always readily available. Local people did not always get the local newsletter, or city newspaper. Many of the mothers who were most extensively involved with the Henley Project believed that informal methods of spreading information were often more effective than relying on local media. Certain agencies and buildings may have a particular reputation which will mean that information coming from there may have less impact, and be treated with suspicion. The involvement of the NSPCC in the Henley Project meant that some parents who worked in it were treated with suspicion, and had to work very hard over a substantial period, through informal networks, to ensure a positive local response to the work. This was backed up by extensive work of members of the Steering Group, local residents, Family Project and other project members, representatives of voluntary and statutory agencies.

Time needed for informed participation is extensive. Often consultative documents can be lengthy and relatively few copies may be provided. Sometimes they may be difficult to get hold of. The development worker thought that some agency representatives were reluctant to make lengthy papers available as they assumed local people would not want to be bothered with such detail. Where such papers were made available — as in the case of Area Management Team papers — local people had been willing to do a great deal of work on them. Extensive copying of these and other documents — e.g. Under 8s Review (1989 Children Act), Community Parks Policy — had allowed considered responses from those who had been able to take them home to study. The involvement in this process of workers with a stated priority to extensive consultation was thought to be crucial.

The timescales of local people and those of officials may not easily be compatible. Local people's motivation may be lessened if they cannot readily get access to an official about a burning issue. Agencies may need up to 2 months warning of any meeting which they need to send a representative to. Convenient times for professional workers may not coincide with parents' responsibilities for collecting young children from nursery or school, or feeding babies. The issue of council officers, particularly those in management positions, spending time with a small number of local residents who may not be representative, is a difficult one. Genuine consultation, involvement, participation and partnership necessarily involve a major commitment of time and different working methods over a long period, which can be difficult to reconcile with other organisational demands.

Towards a partnership culture

In almost every session organised for the Henley Project, questions were raised about the value of local people involving themselves in consultations, providing information, committing themselves to joint work. An enormous number of research and development projects, consultations and attempts to involve local people in new initiatives had taken place over the previous 20 years, leading to a weariness and cynicism in the area. The following comments reflect commonly held views.

What is the point of one more survey.

Telling you won't change anything.

We never know who or what the surveys are for.

There are no results — visible or otherwise. They say they are representative of the area, but only a few people are involved.

People who make decisions about Wood End probably already know about most of the problems and still don't do anything.

People in Wood End have a lot of experience of short term funded projects that come and go so may not feel very keen to get involved in yet another one.

When projects happen, the timetable is out of control.

There is no communication between agencies and the public, resulting in rumours.

Decisions get made then changed without further consultation.

Local residents felt that they were 'in a goldfish bowl' and by making themselves available for research and consultation they could make themselves vulnerable. This was a particular issue when the subject under scrutiny was child protection.

The project worked on a slow and gradual networking approach, using informal community development methods, backed up by supportive resources to enable parents to participate without worrying about childcare arrangements or transport. Not all local workers were convinced that our methods were necessary or useful — some described much of the work as 'a cup of tea and a chat', rather than recognising the slow, painstaking ways in which trust and mutual respect are built up. Much of the groundwork for partnership can be difficult to detect — sometimes the most successful work is the least visible, the least intrusive. The core group of women who continued to meet together, and those involved in the Steering Group and disseminations, believed that it was the quality of relationships, the ways in which their needs as individuals, as mothers and as local residents were taken seriously which were crucial in giving them confidence that they could make a contribution to improving opportunities for children. The style of work, the quality of dynamics and interactions and the structures which were set up to ensure involvement, feedback, careful evaluation, were all key factors. Seeing some results for their efforts and experiencing over a period of two years consistent efforts to maintain their interest and involvement, to support their attempts to improve their own skills, led to the core group of women describing feelings of being valued, working in partnership to improve conditions for their own and other people's children and for themselves. Some of the activities, action and outcomes associated with the work of the project and with other groups working collaboratively with it will be described in the next chapter.

Ownership of research material and sensitivity to parents' and children's needs

From the beginning of the project the emphasis of the research was on quality, rather than quantity, — gaining detailed 'snap shots' of local parents' views and feelings about keeping their children safe from harm. Asking parents to talk about their successes and difficulties in bringing up their children is a sensitive issue, particularly when discussions are focusing on children's safety and protection. The development worker constantly had to ensure that the project's aims, boundaries and respon-sibilities were clear to parents taking part so that they understood the implications of their involvement. Attempts were made to encourage parents to talk about their successes rather than difficulties. Inevitably difficulties would eventually be discussed, but on parents' own terms and after a respectful relationship had been established. All parents and groups were given the opportunity to see the write up of the sessions and to ask for changes to be made.

Sometimes very powerful and significant things were said to the development worker in initial or explanatory meetings with parents, before parents had a clear picture of the project and permission had been gained to document views. Sometimes it was possible to note these comments down and gain permission retrospectively, However this was not always appropriate and respect for the parents' rights and dignity took precedence over collecting the most significant case material. Any child protection concerns were followed up, in line with our clear initial statement about the limits of confidentiality. Whenever this was necessary full discussion was held with parents or workers involved and great efforts made to help them to make any necessary referrals themselves.

The development worker was constantly having to balance the feelings and needs of parents taking part in the project with the project's objective of documenting their views and feelings. Sometimes the development worker would be asked to help parents directly and sometimes to help them gain access to a service. It was not always possible to help them get the help they identified. This was particularly true of intensive counselling services for children and young people, where either *their crisis* was not defined as a crisis by those providing services or there were long waiting lists for a service.

There were often uncomfortable moments and tensions caused by not being able to meet people's immediate needs. However, through the commitment to treating both parents and their children with respect and working with them in an open and honest partnership, it was generally possible to maintain constructive relationships. Local people were very generous in sharing their experiences, even when we could provide little beyond tea and sympathy.

6 Outcomes, future priorities, conclusions

This chapter will review some of the outcomes of the wide range of activities — relevant to the safety and wellbeing of children and families — taking place in the Henley area during the life of the project. It will consider the implications of the findings and experience of the project for planning neighbourhood strategies which may increase the effectiveness of child protection services, reduce harm to children and improve the quality of life for children and their families.

Action during the period of the Henley project

The Henley Safe Children Project was set up for a limited period, to work in partnership with local parents and workers from voluntary and statutory organisations, to document child protection and family support needs in the area, and encourage the development of preventive services. In earlier chapters we have described the findings from the project's work, and how we used these findings. Our work, however, was part of a much wider movement in the area, with a commitment to partnership in evaluating local needs and planning future services. We were engaged with a very wide range of individuals, groups and agencies in a complex process of change.

Community development processes are inherently difficult to monitor and analyse and we would not wish to make any special claims about the influence of the Henley Project on local activities. Action and change arising from the work of a number of diverse groups was substantial during the life of the project. This activity is important, in understanding the project's work and in demonstrating the interconnections of numerous events and processes. In Chapter 5 we drew attention to connections between aims, objectives and process of the Henley work. Here we focus on action related to these, whether directly initiated from the project, or resulting from the work of others.

We should like to acknowledge the many diverse groups who have worked to improve the social environment in the Henley ward since the major expansion of council housing in the 1950s. We do not have access to full information about the activities and views of all influential groups, but would like to draw attention to some of the groups which we consider to have been central to the local developments which we were engaged in.

The National Community Development Project (Benington 1975)

was involved in work in the area in the 1970s, as was Shelter. Their analysis of interconnected problems in the area has been shared by many local people and workers since. Painstaking work had been done by Community Education workers and local groups in identifying local needs and developing participative models of working. These groups were involved in obtaining funding for a purpose built centre and Family Project, set up about the same time as the Henley Project. The Family Project had a wide range of objectives in local neighbourhood support and was committed to partnership with local people. Soon after the Henley Project and the Family Project were set up, the Chief Executive's Department of the local authority set up an Area Management Team (AMT) to manage local authority services for the area and to liaise with health and other statutory services, voluntary agencies and local groups. Its aim was to coordinate action to bring about service improvements and develop a new relationship between local people and the Council. By 1994, the advantages of the area based approach were clear enough for the Council to extend it to other parts of the city. The AMT was concerned with services to all groups in the area. Our focus is more narrowly on services to children and families.

These groups were central to change and activities in the area during the life of the Henley Project and continue to be so. They connect with numerous other groups and agencies which have been active and influential, including probation, a mediation project, community safety initiatives, outreach work from local nurseries, health initiatives and advice work on rights and benefit.

The Henley Project tried to work in close collaboration with all these groups, supporting their initiatives as well as trying to influence their direction, based on our values, theoretical perspectives and findings. They also influenced the direction and outcomes of our work. The Henley development worker had opportunities to be both strategic — through formal connections with these groups in the project Steering Group and later — through the Family Support Group of the AMT — and opportunistic — through her incremental, networking approach, in forging alliances, working jointly with local workers and residents.

The following sections give a brief account of action and changes which relate to the main aims of the project. The work it represents took place against a backdrop of suspicion, mistrust and hopelessness, which local workers and parents claimed resulted from cynicism following many previous consultations and surveys of their views and shrinking resources at a time of increasing pressures on parents and on workers.

Childcare

Following the implementation of the 1989 Children Act, local authorities were obliged to consider the range of services which they should provide for children in their areas who are in need and their family support services. Our work took place against this background. However, resources were very substantially focused on crisis work in the investigation of abuse. Local residents and workers were convinced of the need to increase and improve the availability of affordable childcare, as a major support for children and their carers. There was a huge amount of activity in relation to childcare. The childcare surveys described earlier and follow up work from them led to an expectation locally that parents views on preschool provision would be documented, valued and have some influence on future services. Regular involvement of parents — most usually mothers — became a standard feature in planning under 8s services, in Social Services Department provision and in wider local authority initiatives. A local sub group of the AMT tried to ensure that issues for Black children and their families continued to gain attention.

The need identified by many mothers for flexible, easily accessible preschool provision, led to an emphasis on supporting creche provision. The underuse of the child minding opportunities available — connected to low income — was not easily remedied. Local and city wide groups were active in promoting high quality creche provision, because they believed it could enhance the quality of life for children and their carers. The new and more stringent requirements of the Children Act, however, had led to fears that most voluntary groups would be unable to continue to provide creches. There was fear that many professional childcare workers had a negative view of them.

However the experience of the Henley Project was more positive. Whilst parents were involved in discussions and meetings run by the project their children attended a creche. The creches provided the children with positive preschool experiences of constructive play and activities as well as an enjoyable opportunity to play with other children, on equipment that parents would not normally have available at home. One of the regular creche workers explained her role as

> to give them the freedom to play and enjoy themselves. I try to vary the activities from week to week, for example painting, singing, big and small play.

She continued:

> They tend to go for painting and cutting out which they just love to do, getting messy ... how enjoyable it is to see the children gain confidence, meet other people and their children as well as the development which I have seen in the children ... and parents have noticed that their children are doing well, for example, in speech and playing and they are more open.

Following numerous discussions in the area, a local community creche, to provide carers with occasional breaks from their children, to keep appointments, shop or just catch up on cleaning or sleep, was set up.

A Parent and Toddler self help group was run from the Family Project, open to carers who wanted to 'spend time having fun, while furthering their own relationships with other children/parents'. Community Education workers continued to support a group for mothers of children of mixed ethnic heritage, as well as other outreach activities. 'Drop In' sessions, supported by a free creche, provided social contact, information and discussions at the Family Project. There was also an 'All Sorts Support Group' for parents and carers to meet weekly 'to have time out from kids where they can listen to and support each other'.

Outings and activities for children were supported by a wide range of groups and agencies — for example a summer outing organised by mini cab drivers; summer play schemes funded by NSPCC, by Community Education, and by voluntary and charitable agencies.

Nursery provision of the Social Services Department was highly valued by local parents. Staff had established a strong reputation for supportive, sympathetic work with parents and providing excellent opportunities for the children who had places. Attention to equal opportunities, sensitivity to minority groups was praised. However, there was a continuing general concern from local parents that the Social Services Department's policy of providing places only for families where there were substantial problems led to stigma for those using the provision. Parents associate a place with 'not coping' and with 'child abuse'. African Caribbean mothers particularly expressed a view that 'you have to abuse your child before you get a place'. Cuts in resources have led to closures of nurseries in the city and local parents and workers fear that one of the most constructive services for children and families in need will become set as a crisis, rather than supportive, response.

Family support group

This group, under the auspices of the Area Management Team (AMT) played a central role in agreeing a local strategy for child care and family support services. It was instrumental in ensuring that family support and preventive work were defined as core business of the local authority. The group agreed a strategic plan: 'Before It's Too Late' for a community based preventive family support programme. The programme aimed to enhance 'other existing and developmental work relevant to children's protection, development and wellbeing', particularly 'primary and preschool provision'. Included in the programme were: a befriending service; parenting skills education; a network of support groups; pre crisis counselling; a children's rights project; a young people's advice and information worker; parents' support groups; groups for families, parents and teenagers; children's clubs.

The programme relied heavily on the Family Project to provide an infrastructure. Coordination of effort was central. A directory of under 8s facilities was compiled for agencies and parents. Courses on children's development and on managing behaviour — involving parents as tutors, providing opportunities to gain National Vocational Qualifications — have been coordinated and planned through the group.

New Links Project

As a direct result of the work of the Henley Project the NSPCC agreed to fund this befriending project, as part of the local plan supported by the Family Support Group. The Henley development worker was employed full time to support the work of the New Links Project. A further grant was obtained from the Department of Health Opportunities for Volunteering Initiative, to fund a part time childcare coordinator and a part time volunteer coordinator. The project aims to provide support for parents and children in Wood End, Henley Green and Bell Green. Parents involved in the Henley Project played a key role developing this project and continue to be involved in organising and managing it and in training volunteers. Volunteers support local parents with young children, particularly those more likely to be isolated.

The needs of Black families and of households where a parent or child has a disability are given sensitive and careful attention. Funding is available to meet language and communication needs. Members of the local African Caribbean and Asian communities are represented on the Steering Group and as volunteers. The project regularly gives presentations about its work, particularly about how it managed to involve minority groups, drawing on the work of the Black Access to Childcare Survey and the experience of the Henley Project.

Since the work of the Henley Safe Children Project finished the NSPCC Coventry New Links Project has gone on to address some of the needs identified by local parents. Current core activity includes:

- running a weekly parents/carers group — 'The Together Group', as well as a bilingual Parents' and Children's Group (Hindi, Urdu, Punjabi, English)
- running 2 or 3 'Handling Children's Behaviour' courses a year
- providing a minimum of 52 creches a year
- providing holiday events/activities throughout the year
- providing a one to one weekly home visiting service to parents/carers and their children through trained local volunteers
- providing opportunities for local people who wish to become a Project volunteer through training and supervision
- providing training in child protection procedures, domestic violence, working in partnership with parents, locally, citywide and further afield
- working with a group of local parents/carers who wish to manage the Project, currently working out their own constitution
- keeping up the profile of preventive work and of the interconnected needs of parents/carers and their children; through attendance at appropriate fora and networks

• developing appropriate childcare provision for children with special needs involved in the Project.

This range of services evolved directly from listening to the needs of parents, carers and their children. Parents and carers can readily move between the range of services provided. Parents who come on holiday trips find out about the 'Handling Children's Behaviour Course', or the opportunity to volunteer. Parents attending groups ask for one to one help from a volunteer. Users move on to become volunteers. Volunteers become involved in the management of the Project. Hence parents and carers can enter the Project at different levels, at different times and in different ways. At all levels they have the opportunity to give something to the service, as well as gain something for themselves and their children.

Local parents have continued to be involved in training social work students and social workers on a regular basis, for three local educational institutions. Students and social workers continue to value the opportunity to hear about working in partnership on child protection and prevention from a parents' perspective.

The New Links Project continues the tradition of the Henley Safe Children Project in keeping preventive work firmly on the map. The Project continues to be involved in the local Area Coordination Team, Family Support Group, Domestic Violence Groups, Under 8s work. It is involved in the Early Years Forum set up by the local authority. These ensure that channels of communication are maintained about family support and preventive initiatives amongst groups in the statutory and voluntary sectors. The challenge of involving parents and carers continues to be addressed.

Citywide the Project is represented on the Anti-Poverty Forum — Family Support Working Group and the meeting the Needs of Separating Families Network. Both provide opportunities for discussion about existing provision and gaps which may need to be addressed relating to children's and families' needs.

Although the issue of prevention is more commonly acknowledged than previously, there are still difficulties both locally and citywide about definitions of family support. Discussions take place in a context of cuts in the very services which should be part of a strategic approach to prevention.

This emphasises the importance of continuing attention to process and priorities. The difficulties of achieving integration, coordination and coherence in the face of pressures for targeted and fragmented services persist. Family support work is clearly part of both child protection and preventive work. However discussions of this work are split between the local Area Child Protection Committee (ACPC) where family support is discussed in relation to child protection and the local Anti-Poverty Forum — Family Support Working Group, where family support is discussed in the context of child welfare and safety and more readily seen as prevention.

Both groups use the term family support but it may mean very different things to each group. This lack of clarity is intensified by the fact that different people represent agencies at the different fora. For example, the NSPCC Children's Services Manager attends the ACPC and an NSPCC Project Coordinator attends the Anti-Poverty Forum — Family Support Working Group. People come and go and common understandings may not survive such changes. A strategic approach to discussion and planning of integrated family support services is difficult. Renegotiation of definitions and priorities has to be a permanent feature.

This split has been compounded by a decision to use the local Early Years Forum as the mechanism for consultation over Children's Services planning. The focus for the Early Year's Forum has been on working with under 8s. Family support work is clearly seen as part of this initiative, but is not suggested by the title of the Forum.

Hence preventive family support work has been subsumed under the umbrella of antipoverty work or services to children under 8. Preventive family support initiatives are then relegated to the position of competing for resources with other anti poverty initiatives or a wide range of services to children under 8. They are not readily seen as an essential part of an integrated system of prevention and protection for children and their parents and carers.

Locally, Social Services Under 8s Services are being restructured under a new title of family support work, however because of limited resources, the focus of this work will still be on parents, carers and children who are in crisis. Although the way the services are to be delivered may change, the people who may provide access to them may be more child protection orientated than before.

Play area

Throughout the life of the project, the single most desirable resource for the area which parents identified was a park or safe play area. This ran through all discussion on the project, through surveys and consultations of all kinds. Parents expressed their views in numerous meetings with local authority representatives, through the Area Management Team, through the Henley Project Steering Group and in many other places. The Women's Action for Safety group and other residents' groups put pressure on officers and elected representatives. There was no park in the area and the numerous green areas were considered to be unsafe for children because of their use by older children and youths. Parents consistently expressed their wish to have a safe play area, where they could take their children for leisure and recreation and meet other children and parents in a safe environment.

During the time of the Project, the local authority committed £200,000 for a leisure and play area for Wood End and Henley Green. It was agreed that local parents and young people would be extensively involved in the planning.

Community safety

There were a number of successful initiatives to promote greater safety in the community. These ranged from traffic calming devices such as road narrowing and humps, to cleaning up dangerous rubbish, to local people forming networks of support in reporting criminal activities to the police and resisting intimidation.

Probation, a Mediation Project, Relate, the Family Project, Community Education, local schools and groups were involved in discussions about problems with young people's behaviour, in support for families worried about bullying, and in antibullying campaigns. There were numerous other activities for children and young people, involving local workers and volunteers, such as girls' groups, sport, motor cycle maintenance.

Efforts were being made to plan and coordinate an effective range of local activities through the Area Management Team.

Opportunities for young people

The Community Education Department and Women's Employment Network were active in seeking increased opportunities for education, training and employment, and tying these in with a neighbourhood strategy to combat poverty and increase opportunities.

Information and advice

A local Advice Centre had played a key role in the area in providing information about benefits, helping people gain their entitlements. However, cuts in funding and expectations on the Centre to extend its range of operating made it impossible to provide for the information needs of the area. The 'Drop In' sessions and other activities at the Family Centre showed that there were substantial demands for a wide range of information on counselling services, children's and parents' rights, child protection procedures, health, income, taxation, housing. The Family Project was able to provide a focal point for information exchange to complement the work of the Advice Centre.

The involvement of local people in writing or advising on accessible materials — for example a summary report of the Henley Project and a leaflet about child protection investigations — was crucial in breaking down the professional habits of many groups which did not readily facilitate the spread of information. The inadequacy of formal channels of communication, the importance of personal informal networks, was highlighted by local people. The enormous barriers to communication with groups speaking minority languages, represented by inadequate interpreting and translation facilities, were identified but not yet dismantled. Effective dissemination of information about resources was given priority by the AMT.

The AMT Under 5s Managers Group, Wood End Women's Group, Women's Development Network were all active in spreading information about child care and family support initiatives, safe play areas, community nurseries, health facilities, as well as opportunities for education, training and employment, through written materials and informal networking.

The Housing Department made a flat available locally to use to give information about the Henley Project, to run groups and engage in supportive outreach work.

The Bush Telegraph — a local paper — covering a wide range of news and local information, was available to all households.

The NSPCC set up local training sessions — across agencies — on child protection guidelines. Health and Social Services collaborated in arranging discussions of parents' concerns.

Resource materials about child protection issues and procedures were made available to a wide range of groups in the area. A play was used to stimulate local discussion. A visit from workers of Newpin in London encouraged parents and workers to share imaginative ideas about the most effective local services they could plan. Local community projects, who were concerned about the Child Support Act, and its effect on children and mothers, were put in touch with researchers involved in nationally sponsored work, for which the NSPCC was one of the key agencies.

A forum of voluntary sector organisations was involved in writing about models of good practice for involving local people in the development and delivery of services. They identified a continuing tension between statutory groups, under pressure to achieve results, and some less powerful voluntary groups who see themselves as more committed to and more experienced in community development and partnership models of service.

Difficulties were sometimes experienced in gaining acknowledgement from some of the more powerful organisations about the extent to which their apparently successful consultations and ability to develop self help resources, depended on long term neighbourhood work by other groups, who could be rendered invisible in the accounts given of such work.

It is arguable that the most effective community development work is unobtrusive, sometimes undetectable. Voluntary groups, in describing good models of practice, emphasise that effective work is permanent, continuous. Partnership, involvement, tapping community resources, demands a detailed attention to process, to renegotiation of definitions, expectations, engagement, which statutory organisations have rarely been able to commit. It would appear that successful outcomes in the Henley area were helped by the high level of commitment to participative, developmental approaches, given by a wide range of organisations in the city and locally, during this active period.

Local Authority commitments: the Area Management Team (AMT)

The work of the AMT, begun in 1993, provided a major opportunity for the developing partnership work in the Project area to have a wider influence. The Team aimed, through integrated management, to emphasize community and customer links, interdepartmental working and interagency provision and to improve services in the area through better coordination (Gaster, 1994 and Coventry City Council internal documents). There were eight service areas involved:
  • Employment and training
  • Environment
  • Housing
  • Advice and information
  • Leisure opportunities
  • Community safety
  • Health and community care
  • Community development and involvement

One of the key aspects stressed in an evaluation report (Gaster 1994) was the continuing importance which had to be given to values and cultures of working and of management — consciously developing processes which supported working together, outward looking and community oriented approaches. Another lesson emphasized was that the whole Council needed to be oriented towards consumers and the community; the whole organisation needed to be clear about what 'working locally entails and to be committed and involved in putting it into practice'.

Equal opportunities and empowerment

We tried throughout the life of the Henley project to model good working practices, emphasising the time scales necessary in successfully drawing on community resources, setting up partnerships, in planning, implementation and management. We cannot of course claim always to have succeeded. We consistently argued for attention to equal opportunities issues on an hourly, daily, ongoing basis! Access to buildings for people with disabilities; readily available interpreters; information in different formats and languages; meetings arranged at times which allow attendance by people with caring and work commitments; creches and other caring supports necessary to assure attendance, are some of the practicalities which need to be taken care of if equal opportunities principles are to be taken seriously.

Along with other projects in the Henley area, the Henley Safe Children Project provided an opportunity for parents' views of their needs in bringing up children in the area to be taken account of by many individuals and organisations. Local parents gained confidence in expressing their opinions in a wide range of public presentations, in making demands on public officials and elected representatives. Those whose views were expressed in writing, or described by others, were given regular feedback about their material and what was happening to it. They saw a number of changes in the area which corresponded to the priorities they had identified. We hope that the tireless efforts which they made to provide the best opportunities possible for their children and for those of other people have been adequately acknowledged in our account.

Raising the profile of preventive services

The Henley Project was part of a movement supported by many local residents and workers to raise the level of consciousness in childcare agencies of the key role of childcare provision and family support services in areas of disadvantage. The relentless practicalities, the stresses of caring for children on low incomes in an area of high unemployment, high crime, health problems and other difficulties, place a heavy burden on carers. In the project area the proportion of children and young people to adults was almost twice as high as for the city as a whole. The statistics showing strong links between disadvantage and harm of various kinds, collected and discussed in dissemination activities, gave local parents and workers material to back up their demands for greater priority to be given to prevention and support. There was widespread discussion of this material locally and regionally, with local workers and politicians, in professional seminars, in training events in Social Services and in the two local universities. National charities — NCH Action for Children, Barnardos, Save the Children and NSPCC — were involved in local and national presentations. Findings from the Project and accounts of successful British and American preventive, community wide projects, were presented to Area Child Protection Committees and at national and international conferences.

A number of recent initiatives and reports (Audit Commission 1994; Childhood Matters 1996; Messages from Research 1995; Sinclair et al 1997) have highlighted the gaps in family support and preventive work in child care and protection, echoing findings of the Henley Safe Children Project.

The NSPCC used the experience of the project, along with the findings of other neighbourhood support initiatives, in planning its change of emphasis from crisis oriented services to services where preventive and therapeutic responses to harm and the promotion of wellbeing are equally stressed.

The emphasis on family support, of the Henley Safe Children Project, developed through the NSPCC Coventry New Links Project, has moved from the fringes of child protection work to become core business of the NSPCC and other national initiatives.

Future priorities; conclusions

The common sense view that it is hard to provide a healthy, safe and nurturing environment for children in areas of social and economic disadvantage is well supported by research (Baldwin and Spencer 1993; Tuck 1995; Sinclair et al 1997). A cluster of influences appears to produce a cluster of consequences, with the familiar picture in areas of deprivation of high levels of crime, child abuse, educational failure and truancy, unplanned teenage pregnancies, low birth weight and many other health and social problems. Child abuse and neglect, as well as other aspects of harm to children, are consistently correlated with material deprivation (Sedlak 1993).

Given the demoralisation, alienation and disintegration of relationships which may follow chronic stress arising from deprivation, as well as the major hindrances to health, education and practical functioning which accompany it, it is hard to understand why the balance of resources is still weighted so heavily in favour of individualised crisis responses. The UN Convention on the Rights of the Child, the 1989 Children Act, the 1995 Children Scotland Act; the Audit Commission Report 'Seen but not heard' (DoH 1994) and 'Messages from Research' (DoH 1995) strongly support a change in emphasis — to services geared to supporting families.

Chamberlin (1988) argues the need to target community wide support services on areas where there are substantial, but not overwhelming, levels of risk of harm, as it is more likely that intervention will be effective before the downward spiral is too far advanced. He acknowledges that such an approach will not provide an answer to the most entrenched problems among very high risk groups. Parallel concentration of intensive services on very high risk groups and areas may be necessary in the short term, but should not be allowed to absorb all available resources. Long term impact on safety, wellbeing and quality of life depends on enabling neighbourhoods of medium risk to make progress towards lower risk.

Many women — and a much smaller number of men — were involved with the Henley Project and other groups in the area in building networks of support and in developing resources for families and children. They did however identify many gaps in resources. They also described difficulties in gaining access to existing resources, sometimes because of low income, lack of transport or childcare.

Many parents found it difficult to get the help they needed to cope with the every day demands of shopping, housekeeping, getting children to school, nursery, clinic appointments, spending 'quality' time with their children, taking them on rewarding outings. Although there was a wide range of childcare available in the area, it was organised by many different groups and individuals and was not always flexible enough to cope with unexpected or unplanned needs. Coordination of affordable

child care provision and ready access to information about it was identified as a priority.

Parents documented in detail some of the problems and stresses in
bringing up children in the area. They expressed particular concern that
at times of unexpected difficulty, or personal crisis, *they could not rely
on having access to support services*. The relentless practicalities of
bringing up children could at such times become overwhelming.

The needs which parents identified and the resources which they
and local workers identified as essential in coping with the demanding
task of child rearing were very similar to those which were identified in
chapter two, associated with positive outcomes in other neighbourhoods
where parents were experiencing similar problems: a wide range of readily accessible child care and support services for children and families.

Like many community projects and child care initiatives, work was
heavily supported by the commitment and skills of local women — particularly mothers of young children. We were particularly concerned that
our small scale project had not been able to pay as much attention as was
needed to involving fathers — and other men — in the project. We were
in danger of perpetuating the traditional expectation that it is mothers'
responsibility to shoulder the main burdens of child care. Single mothers
are scapegoated in political and media debate as primarily responsible
for many social problems. The debate about attempting to discourage
lone parenting through withdrawal of benefits takes little account of the
many complex reasons why children are currently being brought up in
single parent households. Cutting financial benefits increases hardship,
stress and likely risks of harm for children. The debate has given insufficient acknowledgment to the central role which single mothers — and
other women — play in maintaining a sense of social responsibility and
order.

This issue ties in closely with a problem identified by parents and
workers associated with the Henley Project, in parallel with the need for
readily available childcare and family support services. Local people
identified an urgent need to work within the community to challenge
and change negative, destructive and discriminatory attitudes and
behaviour shown by some individuals, families and groups. In particular
the behaviour of some groups of young males was identified as problematic.

Ways are needed to change the negative, destructive energy and initiative which some young people in the neighbourhood show, into
positive, purposeful commitment to the area. Although the need for such
work was identified within the agreed neighbourhood strategy, it is
another area where we would have liked the opportunity to give greater
emphasis, to do more work. Much greater attention is needed to the
opportunities to work with young people in the Henley area — and in
similar neighbourhoods — to change the area from one of the most

dangerous places for children and adults, into a safe place to bring children up.

The important role of youth and community services, using outreach, community development approaches, needs continuing emphasis. The destructive, disruptive and criminal behaviour common in some areas of disadvantage can be understood in relation to frustration, alienation and lack of opportunity, but makes the role of parents very difficult. It can however coexist with individual altruism and concern for others. *It seems unlikely that the young people involved in disruptive behaviour in the Henley and other areas would claim any commitment or intention to cause harm to younger children.* Parents involved with the project, however, saw the behaviour of a minority of young people as a major source of difficulty for them in keeping their children safe. Any attempt to change such behaviour will need to be targeted not only on individuals — in schools, youth clubs, on probation and in community education — but through unattached work, alongside young people in the situations on the street and elsewhere where behaviour is at its most problematic (NACRO 1997). The situations in which 'macho' culture is encouraged and perpetuated, the social environment, will need as close attention as family support, if there is to be any lasting improvement.

Participation and partnership (Smith 1995) are likely to be as central to work with children and young people as to work with parents. This will involve listening to and working with young people as experts on their own situations, recognising that behaviour in groups of their peers may be very different from behaviour in other situations. Community development approaches will need to be backed up by opportunities for training and purposeful employment which can encourage feelings of self worth, commitment to making a positive contribution within neighbourhoods and communities.

The implications of the Henley project findings and experience, as well as wider research findings and evaluations (Chamberlin 1988; Schorr 1988; Zigler and Styfco 1993; Sinclair et al 1997), suggest the need for multiagency, long term neighbourhood strategies. These strategies need to be developed in partnerships between local people and voluntary and statutory organisations. They need to have the following elements:

- comprehensiveness; offering a broad spectrum of services, flexible and informal as well as intensive;
- family and community oriented;
- staff with time and skills to develop relationships of respect, trust and collaboration;
- continuity of small committed teams;
- support from organisations for workers to cross boundaries, change roles;
- recognition that needs are untidy, cross professional and bureaucratic boundaries.

Children need to be seen in the context of their families and wider social and cultural environments. Tensions between the rights of children and the rights and needs of their parents, carers, families, need to be recognised. The explicit priority in the Children Acts to the welfare of the child, whilst emphasizing family participation and cooperation, recognises such tensions. Conflicts of interest between different groups need to be recognised and worked with. The three key action points which we would want to emphasise as a result of experience in the Henley Project are:

Family support

- *practical*: childcare — daily, evenings, respite; emergency sitting services; user friendly clinics, surgeries, shops etc; safe play areas; accessible transport;
- *social and emotional*: local social networking; counselling for parents and children, accessible when they say they need it; behaviour management and preparation for parenthood classes;

Social environment

- *attention to*: safe constructive play and activities for all ages; crime, drug abuse, violence, bullying, racism, sexism, prejudice; 'macho' destructive street cultures; negative, alienated behaviour of young people; intimidation of children with disabilities; aggressive assertion of power by white people; male attitudes to power and sexuality.

Partnership, participation, opportunities

- needs led flexible services;
- recognition of expertise of local people, power to identify needs and control resources, using local skills and networks;
- links to training and job opportunities; anti-poverty initiatives, anti oppressive policies and practices.

The major links between deprivation and harm to children and their carers are amply demonstrated. The resulting stresses and long term difficulties were lived realities for parents and children in the Henley area. Whilst recognising that the fundamental problems need major political and economic interventions, nevertheless the worst consequences of disadvantage can be lessened by community and family supports, making it more likely that parents will cope with their own and their children's needs. Such initiatives do not need to mask the extent to which disadvantage underlies many of the problems facing children. Community development, partnership approaches, drawing on local energy and resources, can be effective in raising consciousness of the complex interplay of economic, social and interpersonal factors involved, and can lead to a dynamic regeneration of social relationships and political activity.

Strategies based on national and local data about material resources, social supports and services available to children and families will meet local authorities' responsibilities under section 17 of the 1989 Children Act, as well as upholding the principles of the UN Convention on the Rights of the Child. They will make it possible for the potential for responsibility within communities to be recognised and developed, the needs and strengths of minority groups to be taken account of, the valuable role of mothers in caring for children to be valued and shared, so as to provide effective protection for children and promote their wellbeing as healthy fulfilled and socially responsible members of society.

A challenge for the next millennium is whether support services provided for parents, carers and their children will continue to be prescriptive, reactive, crisis led, working in isolation from users, or flexible, proactive, needs led and working in genuine partnership with users of services, however limited the resources available.

> The relationship between child protection, and family support is complex. The debate about the 'balance' between child protection and family support assumes that these are two competing, or even incompatible, activities and that, in principle, services and social work activity can be refocused from child protection into family support. In fact the relationship between the two is very complex. There are many ways in which these activities may interact and, depending on the specific case, the relationship between the two can change over time. We believe that the refocusing debate should acknowledge these complexities and that simply changing definitions or reallocating resources will be inappropriate and perhaps a dangerous response to the real opportunities that the debate has provided.

> Family support services require active development; child protection processes require active reform. Determined action must follow debate.'(NSPCC 1996)

Messages from parents

It is appropriate to complete our account of the Henley Project as we began it — using parents' own words. This is an extract from a letter sent by four of the mothers who were involved throughout the project:

> We got involved in the Henley Project because we had major concerns about the safety of our children living on this estate. We wanted to talk about out concerns and try to change things for the better.

> As residents of this estate we are often treated by policy makers as second class citizens. This Project gave us the opportunity to have our views valued and acted upon. We were able to present ours and other parents' views to 328 professionals from both voluntary and statutory agencies. We told these

people about the pressures that parents on this estate are faced with every day. These presentations worked well because we all believed in what we were doing, we were able to speak to people that we don't normally get a chance to reach.

Changing attitudes

Being involved in this Project has helped us recognise and value the skills that we already had. We have been encouraged to use these skills to achieve things that previously ourselves and other people would have thought impossible. Our self confidence and self esteem have improved. We now feel able to disagree with people openly, and believe that what we have to say is important and will be listened to.

Support for parents

The NSPCC has responded positively to our views by providing our area with a coordinator and administration time for the New Links Project , Support Opportunities for Parents and Children in Wood End, Bell Green and Henley Green.

As parents we have welcomed the NSPCC's promotion of preventive work in child protection. We believe that only by working in partnership with parents and communities can the NSPCC hope to achieve the prevention of child abuse.

Source: Elaine O'Brien, Nicki Moore, Sam O'Connor, Mandy Watson

In deciding on the contents of a summary report parents involved in the Henley Project were clear about the message which they wanted to give to workers, officials, politicians and other parents:

We have the same fears as professionals for our children — we also have the same expectations for them as everyone else does. We have found that people do care about children but we need support to carry on caring. We want to help professionals to help us.

We are there, use us to help. We don't want you to feel pity for us, we don't want you to think 'Oh! What a shame', when you look at where we live. It's very hard to keep up our expectations for ourselves and our families when living in this environment. We don't need to be patronised or told what to do all the time. We need to have parent support services so our children can be really safe.

Children need to be loved and cared for by their families and the community they live in. They need to be told that they are important and the people they share the community with are important as well.

We all have a responsibility to make children safe.

Appendix

TACT: Training, Action & Care Together Project: East Community Association Sunderland

Key points about participation

Local people are experts about their own neighbourhoods — they live there.

'Professionals' are experts in their own particular fields.

We need to recognise skills, understanding and expertise wherever it lies, irrespective of a person's 'status'.

People must be involved in creating the solutions to the problems which they face.

People want to be part of a caring community *but* there is a limit to the amount of care any community can offer — depending on the burdens that community already shoulders, and the resources made available to support and enable members of the community in their caring role.

Caring is not something done by 'volunteers' but by residents in the community as part of their everyday life.

Participation does not just happen — it must be worked at. This means using the right settings, providing the right facilities e.g. transport, child-care and using a style which allows participation.

It is essential to start where people are at.

Language and local experience of "the system" can be barriers to participation.

Motivation matters. Previous bad experiences/failures can affect motivation. Publicise and give credit for successes.

Listening matters as well as talking.

We need to learn from each other and avoid isolationism, elitism and parochialism. There is life and some good ideas outside Sunderland!

Work must start in small groups.

Recognise people's fears — whether local residents or workers for statutory agencies.

Build on strengths.

Recognise the importance of informal networks.

A good (free) lunch works wonders!

Involving 'The Community' is an on-going, long-term process.

Effective participation is dependent on adequate information.

Issues overlap and cannot be compartmentalised.

Local people must share in the ownership of the policies which are implemented in their area.

Priorities cannot be imposed if they are to succeed — they must be agreed.

Links must be maintained through on-going informal contacts.

Bibliography

Aldgate, J., Tunstill, J. (1994), *Implementing S17 of the Children Act*, University of Leicester and University of East Anglia/NCVCCO

Aldgate J. and Tunstill, J. (1996), *Making sense of section 17*, HMSO, London.

Atkar, S., Ghataora R. with Baldwin, N., Thanki, V. (1997), *Hifazat Surukhia: Keeping Safe. Child Protection and Family Support Needs of Asian Children and Families — Final Report*, NSPCC, University of Warwick, University of Dundee.

Audit Commission (1994), *Seen but not heard?* HMSO London.

Audit Commission (1996), *Misspent Youth: Young People and Crime*, Audit Commission Publishers, Abington.

Baldwin, N. and Harrison, C. (1993), 'Supporting children in need: the role of the Social Worker' in *Working Together for Young Children*, Routledge, London.

Baldwin, N. and Spencer, N. (1993), 'Deprivation and child abuse: implications for strategic planning', *Children and Society*, 7;4.

Barker, W. et al. (1987), *Community Health and the Child Development Programme*, University of Bristol.

Barnard, Booth, Mitchell, Telzrow, (1989), *Newborn Nursing Models*. Final Report Project RO1 NU00719, Department of Health and Human Services, Washington D.C.

Bebbington, A. and Miles, J. (1989), 'The background of children who enter local authority care', *British Journal of Social Work*, 19(5).

Becker, S. and MacPherson, S. (eds) (1988), 'Public issues, private pain', *Social Services Insight*.

Bell, C. and Roberts, H. (eds) (1984), *Social Researching: Politics, Problems, Practice*, Routledge and Kegan Paul, London.

Benington, J. (1975), 'Changing strategies in Coventry Community Development Project', in Lees, R. and Smith, G. (eds), *Action Reserch in Community Development*, Routledge and Kegan Paul, London.

Benington, J. (1994), 'Quality — a central issue for today's councillors'. *Municipal Review & Association of Municipal Authorities News*, March 1994.

Benyon, J. (1993), 'Disadvantage, Politics and Disorder: Social Disintegration and Conflict in Contemporary Britain', *Occasional Paper*, Centre for the Study of Public Order, University of Leicester.

Beresford, P. and Croft, S. (1986), *Whose Welfare? Private Care or Public Services*, Lewis Cohen Urban Studies, Brighton.

Birchall, E. (1989), 'The frequency of child abuse — what do we really know', in Stevenson, O., *Child Abuse*, Harvester\Wheatsheaf, Hemel Hempstead.

Blackburn, C. (1991), *Poverty and Health: Working with Families*, Open University Press, Milton Keynes.

Blackburn, C. (1992), *Improving Health and Welfare Work with Families in Poverty*, Open University Press, Buckingham.

Blaxter, M. (1993), 'Continuities of Disadvantage', in Waterstone, T. (ed), *Perspectives in Social Disadvantage and Child Health*, Intercept Ltd., Andover, N.H.

Booth, R. and Booth, W. (1994), *Parenting under Pressure: Mothers and Fathers with Learning Difficulties*, Open University Press, Milton Keynes.

Brown, G.W. and Harris, T. (1978), *Social Origins of Depression: a study of psychiatric disorder in women*, Tavistock, London.

Brown, M. (1983), *The Structure of Disadvantage. SSRC/DHSS Studies in Deprivation and Disadvantage*, Heinemann, London.

Brown, M. and Madge, N. (1982), *Despite the Welfare State*, Heinemann Educational Books, London.

Burchall, E. (1989), 'The frequency of child abuse: what do we really know?' in Stevenson, O. (ed) *Child Abuse: Public Policy and Professional Practice*. Harvester/Wheatsheaf, Hemel Hempstead.

Campbell, B. (1993), *Goliath: Britain's Dangerous Places*, Lime Tree.

Cannan, C., and Warren, C. *Social action with children and families. A community development approach to child and family welfare*, Routledge, London.

Chamberlin, R. (ed) (1988), *Beyond Individual Risk Assessment: Community Wide Approaches to Promoting the Health and Development of Families and Children*, The National Center for Education in Maternal and Child Health, Washington DC.

Clark, M. (1988), *Children under 5 Research and Evidence*, Gordon & Breach Science, New York, London.

Cook, J. and Watt, S. (1992), 'Racism, Women and Poverty' in *Women and Poverty in Britain* Glendinning & Millar (eds), Harvester/Wheatsheaf, Hemel Hempstead.

Court Report (1976), *Fit for the Future: Report of the Committee on Child Health*, DHSS, London.

Cox, A., Pound, A., Puckering, C. (1992), 'Newpin: a Befriending Scheme and Therapeutic Network for Carers of Young Children' in Gibbons, J. (ed) *The Children Act 1989 and Family Support*, HMSO, London.

Craig, G. and Mayo, M. (eds) (1995), *Community Empowerment: A Reader in Participation and Development*, Zed Books.

Creighton, S. and Noyes, P. (1990), *Child Abuse Trends in England and Wales 1988-90*, NSPCC, London.

Dalgaard L. (1991), 'From Signals to Action: Preventing Child Abuse', BASPCAN National Congress, Leicester.

Dalley, G. (1988), *Ideologies of Caring*, Macmillan, London.

Devore, W. and Schlesinger, E. G. (1987), *Ethnic - Sensitive Social Work Practice*, Merrill, Columbus, Ohio.

DHSS (1980), *Report of a working group on inequalities in health: the Black report*, HMSO, London.

Dingwall, R., Eekelaar, J. and Murray, T. (1983), *The Protection of Children: State Intervention and Family Life*, Blackwell, Oxford.

DOH (1992), *The Health of the Nation:* White Paper. HMSO, London.

DOH (1995), *Child Protection: Messages from Research*, HMSO, London.

Dumaret, A.C., Coppel-Batsch, M., Courand, S. (1997), 'Adult outcome of long-term foster care' in *Child Abuse and Neglect*, 21, No.10, 911–927.

Earls, F., McGuire, J. and Shay S. (1994), 'Evaluating a community intervention to reduce the risk of child abuse: methodological strategies in conducting neighbourhood surveys', *Child Abuse and Neglect*, 5, 473–85.

Farrington, D.P. (1996), *Understanding and Preventing Youth Crime*, Rowntree Foundation, York.

Farrington, D.P. and West, D. (1982), *Delinquency: Its Roots, Careers and Prospects*, Heinemann.

Farrington, D.P. and West, D. J. (1990), 'The Cambridge Study in Delinquent Development: A Long Term Follow Up of 411 London Males' *Kriminalitat* pp. 115-138, Heidelberg.

Finch, J. and Groves, D. eds. (1983), *A Labour of Love: Women, Work and Caring*, RKP, London.

Finkelhor, D. (1986), *Child Sexual Abuse: New Theory and Research*, Free Press, New York.

Freire, P. (1970), *Pedagogy of the Oppressed*. Penguin, Harmondsworth.

Freire, P. (1972), *Cultural Action for Freedom*, Penguin, Harmondsworth.

Garbarino, J. and Sherman, S. (1980), 'High-risk neighbourhoods and high-risk families: the human ecology of child maltreatment'. *Child Development*, 51, pp. 188-98.

Gaster, L. (1994), *Evaluation of the Wood End/Bell Green Area Management Initiative*, School for Advanced Urban Studies, Bristol University.

Gaudin, J.M. Jr. (1993), 'Effective intervention with neglectful families', in *Criminal Justice and Behaviour*, Vol. 20; 1. 66–89.

Gelles, R.J. (1982), 'Problems in defining and labelling child abuse', in Starr, R. (ed), *Child Abuse Prediction*, Ballinger, Cambridge, Mass.

Gibbons (ed) (1992), *The Children Act 1989 and Family Support: Principles into Practice* , HMSO, London.

Gibbons, (1995), 'Family Support in Child Protection' in Hill, M., Kirk, R.H. and Part, D. (eds), *Supporting Families*, HMSO, Edinburgh.

Gibbons, J., Thorpe, S. and Wilkinson, P. (1990), *Family Support and Prevention: Studies in Local Areas*. HMSO/NISW, London.

Gill, O. (1992), *Parenting under Pressure*, Barnardos, Cardiff.

Glucksman, M. (1994), 'The Work of Knowledge and the Knowledge of Women's Work' in Maynard, M. and Purvis, J. (eds) *Researching Women's Lives from a Feminist Perspective*, Taylor and Francis, London.

Gough, D. (1993), *Child abuse interventions: a review of the research literature*, HMSO, London.

Graham H. (1983), 'Caring: a labour of love' in Finch and Groves, *op.cit.*

Graham, H. (1993), *Hardship and Health in Women's Lives*, Harvester\Wheatsheaf, Hemel Hempstead.

Graham, H. and Jones, J. (1992), 'Community Development and Research', in *Community Development Journal*, Vol. 27, 3.

Gulbenkian (1983), *Community challenge:* report of a conference held at Liverpool University, 16th-19th September 1981, Calouste Gulbenkian Foundation, UK Branch, London.

Henderson, P. (ed) (1995), *Children and Communities*, Pluto Press in association with Community Development Foundation, London.

Hiatt, S. (1996), 'The Implementation of Paraprofessional Home Visitation to New Families: Challenges and Opportunities', paper presented at The International Congress for Prevention of Child Abuse and Neglect, Dublin, Ireland.

HMSO (1991), *The Children Act 1989 Guidance and Regulations*, London. Vol. 2.

Holman (1988), *Putting Families First: Prevention and Child Care,.* Macmillan Education in association with Children's Society, London.

Hudson, F. and Ineichen, B. (1991), *Taking it Lying Down: Sexuality and Teenage Motherhood*, Macmillan, Basingstoke.

Kelly, L., Regan, L., Burton, S. (1992), *An Exploratory Study of the Prevalence of Sexual Abuse in a Sample of 16-21 Year Olds*. Child Abuse Studies Unit. Polytechnic of North London.

La Fontaine, J. (1990), *Child Sexual Abuse*. Polity Press, Cambridge.

Macdonald, G. and Roberts, H. (1995), *What works in the early years: effective interventions for children and families in health, social welfare, education and child protection*, Barnardos, Barkingside.

MacDonald, L. and Billingham, S. (1990), *Families and Schools Together, Programme Evaluation*, FAST Project, Madison, Wisconsin.

Mayall, B. (1986), *Keeping Children Healthy*, Allen and Unwin, London.

Mayall, B. and Foster, M-C. (1990), *Child Health Care: Living with Children, Working for Children*, Heinemann Nursing, Oxford.

Maynard, M. and Purvis, J. (eds) (1994), *Researching Women's Lives from a Feminist Perspective*, Taylor and Francis, London.

Mayo, M. (1994), *Communities and Caring: Mixed Economy of Welfare*, Macmillan.

Melton, G.B. and Barry, F.D. (eds), (1994), *Protecting Children from Abuse and Neglect: Foundations for a new National Strategy*, The Guilford Press, New York.

Miller, J.L., Whittaker, J.K. (1988), 'Social Services and Social Support: Blended Programmes for Families at Risk of Child Maltreatment'. *Child Welfare* Vol. 67.

Montgomery, S. (1982), 'Problems in the Perinatal Prediction of Child Abuse', British Journal of Social Work, 12, 189–196.

NACRO *(1997), Families and Crime*, London.

NCB (1987), *Investing in the Future: Child Health Ten Years After the Court Report* National Children's Bureau, London.

NCH Action for Children (1992), *Factfile 92*, NCH Action for Children, London.

NCH Action for Children (1993), *Factfile 93*, NCH Action for Children, London.

NCH Action for Children (1995), *Factfile 95*, NCH Action for Children, London.

NCH Action for Children (1996/7), *Factfile 96/7*, NCH Action for Children, London.

NCH Action for Children (1997), *Fact file 98*, NCH Action for Children, London

New, C. and David, M. (1985), For the Children's Sake, Penguin, Harmondsworth.

NSPCC (1987), *Child Abuse Trends in England and Wales 1983-1987* NSPCC, London.

NSPCC (1990), *Child Abuse Trends in England and Wales 1988–90*, NSPCC, London.

NSPCC (1996), *Childhood Matters: Report of the National Commission of Enquiry into the Prevention of Abuse*, Stationery Office, London.

NSPCC (1996), *Messages from the NSPCC: a Contribution to the Refocusing Debate*, NSPCC, London.

Parton, N. (1985), *The Politics of Child Abuse*, Macmillan, London.

Parton, N. (ed) (1997), *Child Protection and Family Support*, Routledge, London.

Pelton, L.H. (1994), 'The role of material factors in child abuse and neglect', in Melton G.B. and Barry F.D., *Protecting Children from Abuse and Neglect: Foundations for a new National Strategy*, The Guilford Press, New York.

Quinton, D. and Rutter, M. (1984), 'Parents with children in care II. Intergenerational continuities', *Journal of Child Psychology and Psychiatry*. 25, 231–250.

Reading, R. (1997), 'Poverty and the health of children and adolescents' in *Archives of Disease in Childhood* 76, 463-467.

Roberts, H. (ed) (1981), *Doing Feminist Research*, Routledge and Kegan Paul, London.

Roberts, H., Smith, S.J., Bryce, C. (1995), *Children at Risk: Safety as a social value*, OUP, Buckingham.

Roberts, I., Kramer, S., Suissa, S. (1996), 'Does home visiting prevent childhood injury? A systematic review of randomised controlled trials', *BMJ*, Vol. 312, 29–32.

Russell, D. (1986), '*The Secret Trauma: Incest in the Lives of Girls and Women*, Basic Books, New York.

Schorr, L. (1988), *Within Our Reach: Breaking the Cycle of Disadvantage*, Anchor Doubleday, New York.

Sedlak, A (1991), *National Incidence and Prevalence of Child Abuse and Neglect: 1988 Revised Report*, Westat, Rockville, MD.

Sedlak, A. (1993), *Risk Factors for Child Abuse and Neglect in the US*. Paper presented at the 4th European Conference on Child Abuse and Neglect: Acting upon European Strategies for Child Protection, ISP-CAN, Padua, Italy.

Sinclair, R., Hearn, B. and Pugh, G. (1997), *Preventive Work with Families*, National Children's Bureau, London.

Smith, T. (1995), 'Children and Young People - Disadvantage, Community and the Children Act 1989' in *Children and Communities*, Henderson, P., (ed) Pluto Press, London.

Spencer, N. (1996), *Poverty and Child Health*, Radcliffe Medical Press, Oxford.

SSI (1995), *Children's Services Plans: an Analysis of Children's Services Plans 1993-94*, DOH, London.

Starr, R. (ed), (1982), *Child Abuse Prediction*, Ballinger, Cambridge, Mass.

Tennant (1995), *Child and Family Poverty in Scotland: the Facts*. Glasgow Caledonian University and Save the Children.

Thompson, R.A. (1994), 'Social support and the Prevention of child Maltreatment' in Melton and Barry (eds), *op.cit.*

Tuck, V. (1995), *Links between social deprivation and harm to children: a study of parenting in disadvantage*, unpublished PhD. dissertation, Open University.

Tuck, V. (forthcoming), 'Links between social deprivation and harm to children' in Baldwin, N. (ed), *Protecting children: promoting their rights?* Whiting and Birch, London.

Utting, D. (1995), *Family and Parenthood: Supporting families, preventing breakdown*. Joseph Rowntree Foundation, York.

Utting, D., Bright, J. Henricson, C. (1993), *Crime and the Family*, Occasional paper 16. NACRO. Family Policy Studies Centre.

Veit-Wilson, J. (1993), 'Summing Up' in Waterston, T. (ed) *Perspectives in Social Disadvantage and Child Health*, Intercept Ltd., Andover.

Wedge, P. and Essen, J. (1982), *Children in Adversity*, Pan Books, London.

West, D. J. (1982), *Delinquency: Its Roots, Careers and Prospects*, Heinemann, London.

Williams, M. (1996), *Childhood Matters: Report of the National Commission of Enquiry into the Prevention of Abuse*, HMSO, London.

Wilson, H. with Herbert, G.W. (1978), *Parents and Children in the Inner City*, RKP, London.

Wolfe, D.A. (1991), Keynote address: National Congress, BASPCAN Leicester.

Wolfe, D.A. (1991), *Preventing Physical and Emotional Abuse of Children*, The Guilford Press, New York

Wolfe, D.A. (1993), 'Child Abuse Prevention: Blending Research and Practice', *Child Abuse Review*, 2;3, 153–165.

Zigler and Styfco (1993), *Head Start and Beyond* Yale, New Haven.